**Social media star and podcast host REMI CRUZ PARSONS** has spent the past thirteen years sharing her life online, paving the way for content creators today. Along the way, she's built a devoted community of more than six million fans who love following her everyday life. In recent years, she's brought her passion for food and cooking to the forefront, inviting viewers into her kitchen to learn, experiment, and have fun with her. Now, her long-awaited debut cookbook *Let's Get Cooking* finally gives fans the chance to cook her favorite recipes alongside her.

Cooking wasn't always easy breezy for Remi. Long before she was sharing recipes online, she was just a curious kid growing up in a vibrant Korean American household in Southern California, where her mom filled the family table with short ribs, kimchi stew, and other soulful meals that sparked Remi's love of food. When she moved out on her own, she found that the trial and error of re-creating those beloved dishes became a joyful exploration that still shapes how she cooks today.

This book is the kitchen companion Remi wishes she'd had. Packed with fun, approachable recipes that inspire you to get a little adventurous and step outside your comfort zone, *Let's Get Cooking* contains grab-and-go breakfasts like **Galaxy Brownie Overnight Oats**, crowd-pleasing staples such as **Spicy Salmon and Avocado on Crispy Rice** for birthdays, **Bacon Cheese Dip with Fried Pita Bread** for girls' nights, **Garlic Parmesan Chicken Wings** for game nights, decadent sweets like **World's Best Cakey Chocolate Chip Cookies**, and much more!

With recipes for every craving and occasion, mouthwatering photography, and Remi's infectious personality woven throughout, *Let's Get Cooking* will instill the confidence you need to savor the joy of cooking and create connections through food.

# LET'S GET COOKING

**Everyday Meals, Tipsy Favorites and Comfort Food Cravings**

REMI CRUZ

Photography by Jennifer Chong

SIMON ELEMENT

New York   Amsterdam/Antwerp   London   Toronto   Sydney/Melbourne   New Delhi

This book is dedicated to my wonderful viewers. I truly can't believe how lucky I am to have been blessed with such an incredibly loving and supportive community for the past thirteen years—to have learned and grown together with you is something I will never take for granted. Thank you for supporting me throughout all of my endeavors since the start of my career. Never did I think making videos in my room in high school would have led me to this very moment. I love each and every one of you so much and can't wait to continue this journey together.

# CONTENTS

**From Drunchies to Cozy Dinners, Let's Do This . . .**  8
    My Fridge and Pantry Tour  12
    A Korean Cooking Primer  16
    Let's Get Cooking Basics  22
    List of "Favorites"  25

**Take Care of Yourself: Grab-and-Go Breakfasts**  26

**Let's Get Hosting: Bring on the Party!**  56

**Happy to Be Here! Weekend Drunchie Brunches**  114

**My Favorite Korean Dishes**  140

**Unbothered and Cozy: Weeknight Meals**  188

Acknowledgments  243
Index  245

# FROM BRUNCHIES TO COZY DINNERS, LET'S DO THIS....

# HEY GUYS! THIS IS IT! MY FIRST COOKBOOK.

I've been a content creator for the past thirteen years. I discovered YouTube in middle school, which led to an obsession with all things digital. Throughout the process, I built the most amazing community I could have ever imagined. I'm a California-based vlogger with two YouTube channels: @RemLife and @MissRemiAshten; two podcasts: *Pretty Basic* and *Basically Unfiltered*; plus my Instagram account @CookingWithRemi, where I share recipes, taste tests, and more.

I'm a girl who likes food and always has. Long before I picked up my first camera and started my channels, I would watch my mom whip up all kinds of amazing dishes. It wasn't until I was on my own at eighteen and needed to cook for myself that I realized how much I took my mom's cooking for granted. I found myself constantly calling her to walk me, step-by-step, through her recipes. In the beginning I found cooking scary and overwhelming; I often forgot ingredients or added things in the wrong order. But now I know that's how you learn!

Slowly, with practice, I started to find my footing. At first, I cooked simple, no-fail dishes and shared my experience of learning how to cook with my audience, who has been with me from the beginning, watching my growth, cheering me on as I experimented, and often following along from their own kitchens.

With my mom's—and my audience's—encouragement, I started making more complex entrées that involved planning or using more complicated techniques like braising or baking, which evolved into multicourse meals. I soon became more confident in the kitchen, more confident in myself, and more confident in my cooking. It was through cooking that I showed—and still do—my loved ones how much I appreciate them. I'd bake for their birthdays or make them soup when they were sick. Cooking for my friends and family is my love language, and it brings me closer to every one of them. I went from sharing videos of myself cooking in my dorm room to now sharing my original recipes with millions of people. I can't believe what my life has become, and I feel like I need to pinch myself every day!

## Cooking for my friends and family is my love language . . .

Growing up, I was glued to the Food Network with my mom—we were obsessed. I attribute some of my earliest cooking knowledge to the OGs like Ina Garten and Rachael Ray, but my biggest influence in the kitchen has always been my mom, Suz. She doesn't measure, which is how I learned *not* to measure, either. If you watch me cook, you'll notice I tend to eyeball things; I add some of this and lots of that, and I don't always use measuring spoons. Being a little loose in the kitchen is truly the core of my cooking philosophy: you do YOU.

My goal is to make people feel comfortable in the kitchen. I am here to cook alongside you, as so many of you have done with me in my vlogs. For beginners, I want to show you that the kitchen is not as scary as it may seem. I'm not very methodical, and when I cook, I like to go with the flow and cook by instinct. I want you to do the same! Cooking doesn't always have to be so serious, and the kitchen is a place where you can let loose, experiment, try new things, and have fun. For those new to cooking, though, I do recommend following my recipes exactly as written for the best results. Let's say you sub table salt for kosher salt, you are going to have a much saltier (possibly too salty) outcome. If you're more experienced in the kitchen, you'll likely know which ingredients you can swap out. I've also included some of my favorite brands throughout—these are the ones I trust and use regularly in my own kitchen. Feel free to use your preferred brands and ingredients, too.

### Speaking of ingredients, I am a garlic girl. A serious one. When most people would use one garlic clove, I use seven. I am Korean after all.

I also fly through garlic powder and onion powder in my kitchen, and you'll see I add it to almost every dish. It's a pantry staple that I feel adds to the complexity of flavors. I am also a salty-sweet girl. You'll notice when I add something spicy or savory, I usually add a little sugar for balance. Sugar is historically a common ingredient in Korean cooking used to enhance flavor and texture.

You'll find a My Fridge and Pantry Tour (page 12) listing some of my favorite ingredients, which is followed by A Korean Cooking Primer (page 16). I grew up in a Korean American household where we ate Korean food two to three times a week. I've included an entire chapter of my Korean favorites (see page 140). For those ingredients, if you don't have one, say pork belly, my mom always says you can go to an American store and get a pork chop.

I grew up in Orange County, California, which is a predominantly white area. My parents both immigrated from South Korea when they were young, so I had some elements of Korean culture while growing up, but they also assimilated to American culture and those traditions were passed down to my brother and me as well. A large part of my Korean culture was taught to me through food. My younger brother, Shane, hates all Korean food—we joke that he eats only beige food—so my mom would make two dinners on Korean dinner nights. My husband, Cal, one of my favorite people in the world to feed, is from the South with a Midwestern dad, and still can't believe I grew up eating delicious Korean food like Galbi (page 169) on the regular. You'll see lots of fusion in my recipes, which is a direct reflection of me.

### A large part of my Korean culture was taught to me through food.

All the recipes in this book have been tested on friends and family. I absolutely adore hosting, and the one way I've learned to do it successfully with my incredibly busy schedule is to prep everything! It is nonnegotiable. As a type A planner, it helps me look as if I've got it together, even when I feel like I don't.

While I love feeding others, this book is about feeding my own cravings. I get so much inspiration from my travels, visits to restaurants, and fellow influencers, which you'll see reflected in many of my recipes. If you're a RemLife viewer, I wanted all the chapters and recipes to feel as if you're watching one of my vlogs. You may also recognize some of my classic recipes in this book. It was important for me to include the recipes that made me fall in love with cooking. I'm often busy and on the go, so I love a grab-and-go breakfast. I adore hosting, and I am known to throw parties for friends to celebrate the smallest occasion. During a long week of filming and podcasting, I want to make delicious lunches and dinners that don't take too much time, thought, or work. When I am craving some good old comfort food, my first choice is always my favorite Korean dishes to remind me of being home with my family. And when the weekend rolls around, I am either indulging at brunch with friends or lying in bed, hungover after a crazy night out, craving a burger. These recipes all mean so much to me, as do you, and I hope you love them as much as I do. Most of all, I hope this book makes you feel a little more at home in the kitchen.

## So . . . Let's Get Cooking!

# MY FRIDGE AND PANTRY TOUR

A big part of cooking is, of course, the food shopping. I love wandering through grocery stores. When I go shopping with friends, they always end up looking for me, only to find me staring at the shelves in amazement. I love filling my own shelves and fridge with fun condiments and interesting shelf-stable goods, but for day-to-day cooking, these are the basics I *always* have on hand, and you will see them called for on the regular in my recipes. And if you know me, you know I love a good Asian market, too. For more about my must-have Asian ingredients, see my Korean cooking primer (page 16).

## My Fridge

- Bacon
- Eggs
- Fresh garlic
- Fresh tortillas
- Grated cheddar cheese
- Heavy cream
- Kewpie mayo
- Kimchi
- Onions
- Parmesan cheese
- Unsalted butter

## My Pantry

- All-purpose flour
- Black peppercorns
- Chicken bouillon powder
- Cornstarch
- Diamond Crystal kosher salt
- Extra-virgin olive oil
- Flaky salt
- Garlic powder
- Gochugaru coarse chile flakes
- Gochujang paste
- Granulated sugar
- Honey
- Italian seasoning
- Matcha
- Mirin
- Onion powder
- Panko breadcrumbs
- Paprika
- Peanut butter
- Potato starch
- Pure vanilla extract
- Rice vinegar
- Soy sauce
- Sushi rice
- Toasted sesame oil
- Vegetable oil
- White rice

# A KOREAN COOKING PRIMER

If you keep up with my vlogs, you already know how much I love H Mart! Wander into any one of the national Asian supermarket chain's stores and you'll find the best snacks, frozen foods, fresh produce, meats, and so much more. It's my go-to for all things Korean cooking. But don't worry, if you don't have a Korean or Asian grocery store nearby, most local grocery stores have an international or Asian aisle where you can find the many essentials you'll need to whip up Korean dishes at home. If you are interested in building up your Korean pantry, here is my list of essentials.

## Every Korean kitchen needs . . .

### Gochugaru Coarse Chile Flakes

Gochugaru is ground-up dried red Korean peppers and is a classic Korean ingredient that adds a spicy punch to any of your dishes. You will find this ingredient available in different levels of coarseness, so make sure to use the correct size; otherwise, your dish might end up WAY too spicy (you'll get a lot more spice in a teaspoon of ground pepper than a teaspoon of coarse flakes!). Together with gochujang, these two ingredients are the backbone of almost all spicy Korean cooking.

### Gochujang Paste

Another classic Korean ingredient, gochujang is a condiment made from Korean red chili peppers, glutinous rice powder, fermented soybeans, and salt. It's spicy, but not too spicy, and adds just the right amount of heat to any Korean dish. A spoonful is fabulous for adding depth to a dish; the paste is even good eaten on its own. I have many memories of my mom slicing cucumbers into spears and serving them with a tub of gochujang on our kitchen table as a refreshing afternoon snack. I especially like the O'Food brand.

### Kimchi

Kimchi is the most classic and traditional banchan, small side dishes that are often set in the middle of the table at a Korean meal to be shared. Kimchi is a fermented spicy cabbage side dish that can be eaten alone or turned into pancakes, stews, and so much more. I guarantee most every Korean household will have kimchi in their fridge. I grew up with parents who had a second fridge devoted to kimchi and all of our other banchans. Kimchi is delicious, but the fermented smell can get pretty intense, so a second fridge ensures your other foods don't start to smell like kimchi!

## Mirin

Mirin is very similar to rice wine vinegar, but due to a high sugar content, it doesn't have the tanginess of rice vinegar. It's similar to sake with a lower alcohol content, and the fermentation process gives it a complex flavor.

## Plum Extract Syrup

Plum extract, made from Korean plums, is a less commonly used ingredient, but when I do use it I can tell a difference in the flavor of a dish. It's a Korean syrup with a little acidity and a little sweetness.

## Rice Vinegar

A by-product of rice wine, rice vinegar has a delicate, slightly sour, almost sweet flavor that adds a nice acidic zing to dishes.

## Soy Sauce

A classic staple ingredient in Asian cooking, soy sauce, made from fermented soybeans, adds a salty, umami depth of flavor to whatever you are cooking.

## Toasted Sesame oil

Toasted sesame oil is an absolute staple in my household. Whether you're adding it to something simple or something complex, toasted sesame oil will take your dish to the next level. The toasted element adds so much depth of flavor to whatever you're cooking, and a little goes a very long way.

# LET'S TALK ABOUT MEAT, KOREAN-STYLE

### Flanken versus English-Style Short Ribs

Short ribs have become synonymous with a special occasion or comforting holiday in our house because they are succulent, flavorful, and some may even say decadent. Beef short ribs are a cut of meat that comes from a cow's rib cage. Short ribs are traditionally cut in two different ways, flanken, also called Korean-style, or English-style. A flanken-style rib, which is thinly cut (about a ½ inch or so) across the bone, is what I tend to use most and is traditional for Korean cooking. English-style ribs are longer, sometimes up to 6 inches, and are cut parallel to the bone. The meat tends to be thicker on this cut and is usually cooked low and slow (Galbi-Jjim, page 171), like a braise, as opposed to flanken, which is often marinated and grilled (Galbi, page 169).

### Pork Belly

If I could, I would eat pork belly every day of my life, but my doctor told me it's not a great idea. However, I still eat it from time to time. Pork belly is exactly what the name implies; it's meat from the belly of a pig. Bacon is made from pork belly—the outer layer of fat is stripped and then the meat is cured and smoked. I use raw, uncured pork belly in some of my recipes, like my luscious Rosé Udon with Crispy Pork Belly (page 161) and Cheesy Kimchi Pork Belly Panini (page 166), which can be a little more difficult to source at mainstream food markets. You can always find it in Asian grocers, though. H Mart has so many types it may be overwhelming. You'll find it in slabs, slices, skin on, skin off, and more. I always specify in my recipes exactly what type you'll need for that reason.

There are two cooking techniques that I want to highlight before we begin because I return to them again and again, both IRL and in the book, and I can get a little more in-depth with you about them here. Similarly, I include three recipes for pantry basics that you'll see used in quite a few of my recipes. So let's get to it!

## Let's Boil Eggs

I love eggs. Period. Eggs are my favorite food of all time. I eat them plain. I eat them as a topper. I eat them just for a snack. I've taught Cal to make eggs just how I like them, so a soft-boiled egg can be waiting for me when I come home.

To make hard-boiled eggs: In the bottom of a large pot, place your eggs in a single layer. Fill the pot with enough water to cover the eggs by 2 inches. Put the pot over high heat and bring the water to a boil, then remove the pot from the heat and cover. Allow the eggs to sit in the water for 13 minutes. Meanwhile, prepare an ice bath (a bowl large enough to hold your eggs with water and ice). After the eggs have rested in the water, drain them, transfer them to the ice bath, and let them sit in the water for 5 minutes. Drain and peel. Store unpeeled hard-boiled eggs in the refrigerator for up to 1 week.

To make soft-boiled eggs (the center will be jammy, not runny): Fill a medium pot three quarters full with water, and over high heat, bring the water to a boil. Prepare an ice bath. Once the water comes to a boil, using a slotted spoon, lower your eggs into the water and reduce the heat to a simmer. Let the eggs cook for 7 minutes and using a slotted spoon, immediately transfer the eggs to your ice bath and allow them to cool to the touch. Once cooled, peel your eggs and eat or use them as a topping or in my Savory Surprise Breakfast Muffins (page 41). Store peeled soft-boiled eggs in the refrigerator for up to 3 days.

## Let's Deep-Fry

I understand deep-frying can be daunting. However, if you relax and have all your tools ready, it really can be quite easy. First, you don't need fancy equipment for deep-frying. A simple pot on the stovetop works well. I prefer to shallow-fry more than deep-fry in most cases. The difference between the two is that when you deep-fry, you completely submerge the food you are cooking in oil (and it requires more oil). On the other hand, when you shallow-fry, the oil only comes halfway up the food (usually you need about a ½ inch of oil in the pan). Deep-frying is better for thicker foods, such as my Fried Crab Rangoons (page 91) or Garlic Parmesan Chicken Wings (page 95). I like to use a large, high-walled pot or Dutch oven when deep-frying that can hold enough oil so there's still plenty of room left in the pot when the food is completely submerged. I like to shallow-fry thinner, more delicate foods like chicken cutlets (see page 233) or chicken tenders (see page 213) in a skillet.

I find using a candy thermometer or digital thermometer is key to regulating the oil temperature. If the oil is not hot enough, the coating can get soggy. And if the oil is too hot, the exterior can cook too quickly while the interior undercooks. The ideal temperature for deep-frying is usually around 350°F to 375°F.

If you don't have a thermometer, you can test the oil by dropping in a crumb of bread or panko. The oil is hot enough if it sizzles and floats to the top. If it sinks and no bubbles form, it's not hot enough. You can also test the oil temperature by dipping a dry chopstick into the oil. If bubbles continuously form around the chopstick, the oil is hot enough.

Two other important tips are:

- Use an oil with a high smoking point, such as vegetable or canola oil.
- Don't overcrowd the oil with food because it can significantly lower the temperature of the oil.

It's important to maintain an even temperature when frying so the food cooks evenly.

### Let's Make Hot Honey

If you don't have hot honey in your pantry but have honey and chiles or pepper flakes, it takes little effort to make your own!

To make hot honey: In a small saucepan over medium heat, stir together 1 cup honey and 3 tablespoons crushed red pepper flakes or 2 hot chiles such as Fresno or Thai and cook until the mixture comes to a gentle simmer. Reduce the heat to low and allow the mixture to cook very slowly for 30 minutes. After this time, test to see if the honey has reached your desired spice level. (I put a spoonful of honey in the fridge to cool it down before testing.) If not, you can add some more pepper flakes. After the honey has been infused, strain using a fine-mesh strainer, stir in 1 tablespoon apple cider vinegar, if desired, and store in an airtight lidded jar at room temperature.

### Let's Make Sweet Sriracha Mayo

When I first lived on my own, I went through a big sriracha phase. Sriracha was my gateway to spicier foods. Mixing sriracha with mayo takes the super-spicy edge off, and, to me, is the perfect combination of creamy and tangy. I like to whip up my own sriracha mayo, but you can always buy it premade in stores.

To make sweet sriracha mayo: In a small bowl, combine ⅓ cup Kewpie mayonnaise (or your brand of choice), 4 tablespoons sriracha, 2 teaspoons granulated sugar, 2 pinches kosher salt, and a pinch of freshly ground black pepper. Stir to combine. Store in a lidded jar in the refrigerator for up to one week.

### Let's Make Breadcrumbs!

I usually have panko for breading on hand, but when I don't, I make my own breadcrumbs. Also, instead of throwing away stale bread, you can make breadcrumbs and freeze them!

To make breadcrumbs: In the bowl of a food processor, pulse 10 slices of stale bread until coarse and crumbly. (I like to leave the bread bag open overnight to ensure the bread is stale; if you're in a hurry, you can toast fresh bread in the oven at 250°F for 10 to 15 minutes and let it cool before putting it in the food processor.) You'll get about 5 cups of breadcrumbs from 10 slices of bread.

# LIST OF "FAVORITES"

I say "this is my favorite" about pretty much everything, but the following really are my all-time *favorite* favorites, plus one of Cal's:

- Eggs are my favorite food of all time.
- My favorite breakfast flavors are the combo of salty, smoky bacon and rich, creamy cheese.
- Cal's favorite food group is breakfast burritos (see page 31).
- My favorite Parsons family holiday tradition is a Taco Bell breakfast.
- Cal's Salted Caramel Cold Foam Espresso Martini (page 60) is one of my favorite "Cocktails with Cal" original recipes.
- Party-Pleaser Goat Cheese–Stuffed Dates (page 71) rank high as a family favorite appetizer.
- Super-Easy Slow Cooker Meatballs (page 85) are a game-day favorite (see my favorite holiday menus, too, on page 64).
- Best-Ever Garlic Butter Rolls (page 89) are an absolute favorite for any party I throw.
- Garlic and cheese are perhaps two of my most favorite additions to any dish.
- Out-of-This-World Galaxy Brownies (page 105) are a twist on a childhood favorite.
- If I had to choose my favorite type of cookie, it'll always be a sugar cookie (Brown Butter Sugar Cookies, page 109).
- Cinnamon's, a sweet mom-and-pop spot on O'ahu, Hawaii, is one of my favorite restaurants.
- Tteokbokki (Spicy Stir-Fried Rice Cakes) (page 145), is one of my all-time favorite Korean dishes.
- Spam is just my favorite (see Kimchi Fried Rice with an Egg, page 165).
- If you make Galbi (Marinated Short Ribs), (page 169), I swear they are going to become your new favorite Korean meal!
- Sweet and Spicy Gochujang Meatballs (page 179) are truly one of my favorite recipes in this book.
- Korean Fried Chicken Sandwich with Asian Pear Slaw (page 181) is hands-down my team's favorite recipe in this book.
- Bang Bang Chicken & Shrimp is my favorite entrée at the Cheesecake Factory—and my Coconut Curry Shrimp & Chicken Bowl (page 239) is my take on it.

*Here we go!*

## Take Care of Yourself

# GRAB-AND-GO BREAK

Those of you who watch my vlogs know I pretty much never skip breakfast—after all, it's the most important meal of the day! As much as I love a leisurely morning spread, given the choice, I'd rather get a little more sleep than wake up and cook. All the recipes in this chapter can be made ahead, so if you're a night owl like me, maybe consider prepping morning meals before bed. Even the smoothie in this chapter can be portioned out, then in the AM you only need to add frozen fruit and blend. Having a premade meal to grab and go is a form of self-care that always starts my morning off on the right foot. From egg bites (see page 43) to apple pie turnovers (see page 33), all these breakfasts guarantee a deliciously sparkly boost to the start of your day.

Korean Short Rib (Galbi) Breakfast Burritos   31
Apple Pie Breakfast Turnovers   33
Quick & Easy Monkey Bread Muffins   36
Savory Surprise Breakfast Muffins   41
Get Your Gains Sausage Egg Bites   43
Chocolate-Covered Strawberry Smoothie   47
Hot Girl Coconut Chia Pudding   49
Galaxy Brownie Overnight Oats   51
Bacony Cheesy Eggy Crunchy Breakfast Wrap   52

I grew up in a house that always had leftovers, which often included my parents' famous galbi, Korean-style short ribs marinated in a sweet and savory sauce (see page 169). It never occurred to me to use galbi in a burrito—until I spotted it on the menu at Erewhon. This is my take on their Spicy Korean Short Rib Burrito but for breakfast. My husband Cal's favorite food group is breakfast burritos, and he gave this one his official stamp of approval. If you don't have leftover galbi, feel free to use whatever protein you have on hand: chicken, beef steak, pork, or even tofu. You could also sub in some cooked veggies or fry up some hash browns to throw in. Honestly, this burrito can stand on its own with the eggs, cheese, and kimchi slaw. I'm OBSESSED.

# KOREAN SHORT RIB (GALBI) BREAKFAST BURRITOS

### Makes 3 burritos

**FOR THE KIMCHI SLAW**

2 tablespoons Kewpie mayo

1 tablespoon sriracha

1 tablespoon apple cider vinegar

1 teaspoon soy sauce

½ teaspoon toasted sesame oil

½ teaspoon granulated sugar

½ teaspoon gochugaru coarse chile flakes (optional)

1 packed cup (about 4 ounces) shredded red or green cabbage (I like to buy the pre-shredded kind in a bag)

⅓ cup (about 2 ounces) finely chopped kimchi

**FOR THE BURRITOS**

3 (10-inch or larger) burrito-size flour tortillas

¾ cup shredded mozzarella cheese

3 large eggs

**1.** Make the kimchi slaw: In a medium bowl, whisk together the mayo, sriracha, vinegar, soy sauce, sesame oil, and sugar. Taste, and if you want it spicier, whisk in the gochugaru. Add the shredded cabbage and kimchi and, using a spatula, toss until well combined. Set aside.

**2.** Make the burritos: Heat a large nonstick skillet over medium-high, then reduce the heat to medium once it's hot. Working with one tortilla at a time, warm it on each side, about 15 seconds, then flip it again and sprinkle one-third of the cheese evenly across the center of the tortilla and continue to cook until the cheese melts, another minute or so. Transfer the warm tortilla with the cheese to a cutting board or baking sheet and repeat the process with the remaining 2 tortillas.

**3.** In a medium bowl, whisk the eggs until the whites and yolks are combined. Add the cream and a few pinches of salt and 1 to 2 pinches of pepper and whisk again.

**4.** In the same nonstick skillet over medium heat, melt the butter and swirl it around to coat the pan, then pour the eggs into the middle of the pan and quickly sprinkle the green onions over the eggs.

*(recipe and ingredients continue)*

3 tablespoons heavy cream

Kosher salt

Freshly ground black pepper

1 tablespoon unsalted butter

2 green onions (green parts only), chopped

1½ cups (about 8 ounces, which is meat from about 4 to 5 ribs) cooked, deboned, fat-trimmed Galbi (page 169), cut into bite-size pieces

1 avocado, sliced (optional)

• • •

**5.** Using a rubber spatula, slowly stir the eggs, scraping the mixture so it doesn't stick. As large, soft curds start to form, reduce the heat and slowly flip the eggs to preserve the curds. As soon as all the liquid egg is cooked, transfer the scrambled eggs to the warmed tortillas, dividing the eggs evenly between the tortillas on the lower third of the tortillas.

**6.** Next, divide the Galbi among the tortillas, then the slaw and, if using, the avocado. Be careful not to overfill; a good rule of thumb is about ½ cup of filling per burrito.

**7.** Fold the left and right sides of the tortilla over the filling, then fold the bottom (the edge closest to you) up over the filling, tucking it in slightly as you roll. Continue to roll the burrito away from you, keeping the sides tucked in and gently tightening the burrito by pulling it back toward you to ensure it stays compact. Serve and enjoy.

**8.** For make-ahead meals, store the burritos in an airtight container, resealable bag, or wrapped in plastic or foil in the refrigerator for up to 1 week. To reheat, wrap the burrito in a damp paper towel, set it on a plate, and microwave on high for about 2 minutes, or until heated through. You can also warm it in a skillet over medium heat, a few minutes on each side, until it's heated through.

My mom is big on pie. She served pie at every holiday. And guess what? Growing up, I DID NOT LIKE PIE. As an adult, though, I do! They say your taste buds change as you get older, so I guess mine have. These turnovers remind me of my childhood faves, like Pop Tarts and Toaster Strudels, crossed with a pie, but a little more elevated. If you're not a fan of apples, go ahead and switch them out for another fresh fruit such as peaches or pears. You could also use blueberries or raspberries, but then omit the cinnamon and water when cooking them down. You'd need to play around with the filling if you go the berry route—you want it somewhat juicy but not overly runny. If that sounds intimidating, you could try a spoonful or two of berry jam in place of the apples. Anyone familiar with my cooking style knows I like to throw in a little of this and a lot of that, so I encourage you to do your own thing, too. I love the idea of making these on a leisurely Sunday with a football game on in the background and then refrigerating them for the week ahead. To eat, I just pop them in the toaster or air fryer on a busy weekday morning.

# APPLE PIE BREAKFAST TURNOVERS

### Makes 8 turnovers

- 4 tablespoons (½ stick) unsalted butter, divided
- 3 Granny Smith apples, peeled and finely diced (about 4 heaping cups)
- ½ cup granulated sugar, plus more for sprinkling
- 2 teaspoons ground cinnamon
- 1 teaspoon pure vanilla extract
- Kosher salt
- ½ cup water
- All-purpose flour, for dusting
- 1 box of 2 crusts (14 ounces) refrigerated pie crust dough, thawed

**1.** Preheat the oven to 400°F. Line a rimmed baking sheet with parchment paper. Set aside.

**2.** In a skillet over medium heat, melt 2 tablespoons of the butter. Stir in the apples, sugar, cinnamon, vanilla, and a pinch of salt. Cook the mixture, stirring occasionally, until the apples are soft and the sauce starts to thicken slightly, about 6 minutes. Add the water and increase the heat to medium high. Stir and cook the apples until the mixture thickens again and starts to look like caramel, another 4 to 6 minutes. Remove the apple filling from the heat and let cool.

**3.** Onto a lightly floured surface, roll out one of the thawed pie crusts and stack the second crust on top of it. Using a pizza cutter or knife, cut the dough rounds into 4 equal quadrants so you get 4 triangles out of each round (8 triangles total). Feel free to experiment with shapes by cutting the dough into pairs of triangles (as pictured), squares, or half-moons to form your turnovers, too. Just note you may have a different yield.

*(recipe continues)*

• • •

**4.** Holding a dough triangle in your hand, add 2 tablespoons of the apple filling to the center and fold it in half the long way, so the edges match up, and pinch to seal. (If the edges don't seal, dab a little water on the edges, then try again.) You don't want to overfill the turnovers as it will make them hard to seal.

**5.** Put the filled turnover on the prepared baking sheet, and, using a fork, press down around all the edges to ensure that they are sealed, then poke small holes in the top to allow steam to escape while baking. Repeat until all the turnovers are filled and sealed.

**6.** Melt the remaining 2 tablespoons of butter, and, using a pastry brush, coat the tops of the turnovers. Sprinkle with sugar and bake until golden brown, 14 to 16 minutes.

**7.** Let the turnovers cool slightly before serving. Turnovers can be stored in an airtight container at room temperature for up to 2 days. To serve, reheat the turnovers in a toaster, in the oven, or in an air fryer at 350°F until warmed through.

## LET'S GET EVEN SWEETER!

For a sweet finish, whip up a glaze to drizzle or pipe over your turnovers. In a small bowl, whisk together 1 cup powdered sugar, 1 tablespoon milk, and 1 drop pure vanilla extract until smooth (add more milk as needed). Drizzle the glaze over the cooled turnovers (otherwise it'll melt right in, which is fine, too; it depends on the look you're going for). If you are feeling fancy, you can put the glaze in a small plastic bag, snip off the teeniest corner, and pipe some decorative squiggles on the turnovers.

I learned how to make this fast yet indulgent treat in high school when I would whip them up at sleepovers with my song and dance team. These portable breakfast bakes are very kid-friendly, and in fact, they are fun to make *with* kids. My nephew Holden is a little too young to get in the kitchen yet, but best bet when it's time, he will be churning these out with me for the whole family! Shaking the store-bought biscuit dough pieces (yep, I like to pop open that can) in a bag with the cinnamon coating is an unexpected technique that little bakers seem to enjoy; it's kind of like playing with your food, your hands will be covered with buttery cinnamon (go ahead, lick your fingers!). Full transparency: You can easily coat the biscuit pieces in the bowl if you don't have a bag. You can also drizzle them with homemade icing to take these to the next, sweeter level.

# QUICK & EASY MONKEY BREAD MUFFINS

### Makes 8 muffins

Baking spray
½ cup granulated sugar
6 tablespoons unsalted butter, melted
2 tablespoons heavy cream
1 tablespoon ground cinnamon
1 teaspoon pure vanilla extract
⅛ teaspoon kosher salt
1 (16-ounce) can biscuit dough (I like Pillsbury Original Grands)

### LET'S GET EXTRA!

For an extra sweet topping, whip up a Powdered Sugar Glaze to drizzle over your muffins.

In a small bowl, whisk together ¾ cup powdered sugar, 3 tablespoons heavy cream, 2 tablespoons melted butter, ¼ teaspoon ground cinnamon, and a pinch of kosher salt until smooth. Lightly drizzle over your muffins or serve in a bowl for dipping your pull-apart muffins into. For a thinner glaze, stir in more cream.

1. Preheat the oven to 350°F. Using a 12-cup muffin tin, coat 8 cups with baking spray. Set aside.

2. In a small bowl, whisk together the sugar, butter, heavy cream, cinnamon, vanilla, and salt until smooth. Transfer the mixture to a gallon-size resealable bag.

3. Using a sharp knife or scissors, cut the biscuits into ¾-inch cubes. (I stack the biscuits and cut 2 or 3 biscuits at a time into 16 pieces.)

4. Pull the biscuit pieces apart and put them into the bag with the cinnamon coating. Seal the bag and shake to distribute the mixture evenly over the biscuit cubes.

5. Open the bag and pull out a chunk of coated biscuit cubes. They will likely stick together. Pull the pieces apart to make sure each one is fully coated before you put them into the muffin cup. Fill each cup just below the rim with biscuit pieces.

6. Bake until the tops turn a dark golden brown, 16 to 18 minutes.

7. Let the muffins cool for a few minutes, then using a spoon or small spatula, pry each one out of the muffin tin. If desired, serve with Powdered Sugar Glaze (see Let's Get Extra!). While the muffins are best eaten right away, they may be stored in an airtight container for up to 2 days.

These muffins are seriously impressive: they are loaded with all my favorite breakfast flavors (ofc bacon and cheese), and they have a delicious (and IG-worthy) surprise inside. It's a whole egg (although you probably guessed it from the photo)! I first got the idea from the San Francisco bakery Craftsman & Wolves, who was promoting their "The Rebel Within" muffin, and ever since I've been obsessed with making my own. I've never been there, so this version is what I imagine the muffin to be (and with my spin because it seemed a little one-note—I'm the kind of girl who likes my pizza with thirty toppings, not just one, so I took the same approach with this muffin and stuffed it to the brim). It may sound complicated, but I promise, it's easier than it seems. These are perfect for your next brunch, both for their wow factor and their taste. They also work well for weekday breakfasts as they keep for a few days and are easy to reheat.

# SAVORY SURPRISE BREAKFAST MUFFINS

### Makes 8 muffins

Baking spray

3 tablespoons vegetable oil, divided

8 ounces (about 8 slices) turkey bacon, cut into small pieces

1 medium yellow onion (about 1 cup), finely chopped

1½ teaspoons kosher salt, plus more for seasoning

⅛ teaspoon freshly ground black pepper, plus more for seasoning

2 cups all-purpose flour

1 teaspoon baking powder

1 teaspoon baking soda

1 teaspoon garlic powder

1 cup whole milk, room temperature

2 large eggs, room temperature

4 tablespoons (½ stick) unsalted butter, melted

¾ cup shredded cheddar cheese

3 green onions (green parts only), chopped (about ½ cup)

8 soft-boiled eggs (page 23), peeled

Hot sauce, for serving

**1.** Preheat the oven to 350°F. Using a 12-cup muffin tin, coat 8 cups with baking spray.

**2.** Heat 1 tablespoon of oil in a large skillet, over medium high heat, until it shimmers. Add the turkey bacon and onion and cook, stirring frequently to prevent sticking, until the onion is translucent and the bacon starts to brown on the edges, 8 to 10 minutes. Season with a pinch each of salt and pepper. Set aside to cool.

**3.** In a large bowl, whisk together the flour, baking powder, baking soda, garlic powder, salt, and pepper. Set aside.

**4.** In a smaller bowl, whisk together the milk and eggs. Make a well in the center of the dry ingredients and pour in the milk/egg mixture. Then pour in the butter and the remaining 2 tablespoons of oil, and, using a rubber spatula or wooden spoon, stir until most of the dry ingredients are wet (this is a very thick batter). Sprinkle in the cheese, the cooked bacon/onion mixture, and the green onions and stir until just combined and no more dry ingredients remain (you don't want to overmix here).

*(recipe continues)*

● ● ●

**5.** Next, put a heaping tablespoon of batter into each of the prepared muffin cups. As best as you can, create a small well in the batter for each cooked egg to sit in. Using your hands, cover the egg with about 3 tablespoons of batter; it'll be a mound rising out of the muffin cup. Bake until the muffin tops start to turn a golden brown and a toothpick inserted into the side of one comes out clean (if you insert it in the middle, you'll hit the egg!), about 20 minutes.

**6.** Serve warm with hot sauce. The muffins may be kept in an airtight container in the refrigerator for up to 3 days. To reheat, wrap each muffin in foil and warm in a 350°F oven until just heated, about 8 minutes. (Keep in mind, the longer you reheat, the harder the soft-boiled egg's center will become.)

### LET'S GET CREATIVE!

The preboiled eggs for the surprise center can be whatever doneness you prefer—soft boil, medium boil, or hard boil! Keep in mind that the eggs will cook a bit more in the muffins, so the end result may also be a surprise.

Feel free to switch up the turkey bacon for pork bacon, finely cut sausage pieces, or other protein of your choice. You could even sub in some greens or vegetables. You could also switch up the cheese, maybe try mozzarella or Monterey Jack. And the green onions, if you don't have them, don't worry. The muffins are still delish without them.

LET'S GET COOKING

To me, this is the perfect healthy grab-and-go breakfast. My friends love coming over and seeing a big container of these in the fridge. You get a nice hit of greens plus eggs, cottage cheese, and sausage for a good dose of protein. Whipping the cottage cheese makes these bites creamier, as does cooking them in a hot water bath—or bain-marie, if we're talking culinary terms. It does take a little more time to cook the eggs this way, but I think it's worth it as I'm a textural person and love the custardy result. If you're tight on time or don't have an extra pan, feel free to bake these egg bites without the water. They'll still be tasty, just not quite as creamy.

# GET YOUR GAINS SAUSAGE EGG BITES

### Makes 16 bites

Baking spray

10 cups water

1 to 2 tablespoons extra-virgin olive oil

1 large red bell pepper, cored, seeded, and finely diced (about 1 cup)

½ medium sweet onion, finely diced (a generous ½ cup)

8 ounces thin chicken & apple sausage links, cut into ½-inch rounds

1 (5-ounce) bag baby spinach, chopped

½ teaspoon kosher salt, divided

¼ teaspoon freshly ground black pepper, plus more as needed

16 ounces (2 cups) low-fat cottage cheese

8 large eggs

1 teaspoon onion powder

1 teaspoon garlic powder

**1.** Preheat the oven to 350°F. Coat a 12-cup muffin tin with baking spray. In a large pot, over high heat, bring the water to a boil. Heat 1 tablespoon (or enough to very thinly coat the bottom of the pan) of olive oil in a large skillet, over medium heat, until it starts to shimmer. Add the bell pepper and onion and stir to coat with the oil for 1 to 2 minutes. Add the sausage and cook until the bell pepper and onion just become soft and translucent and the sausage has cooked through, another 6 minutes or so.

**2.** Add the spinach to the pepper/onion/sausage mixture and stir to combine, cooking until the spinach has wilted, about 2 minutes. Add ¼ teaspoon of salt and a few grinds of black pepper and stir to combine. Remove the skillet from the heat and let the mixture cool for 10 to 15 minutes.

**3.** Put the cottage cheese in a food processor and run on high until smooth and creamy, about 2 minutes (a blender works, too!). Set aside.

**4.** Crack the eggs into a large bowl and whisk together. Add the onion powder, garlic powder, the remaining ¼ teaspoon of salt, and the ¼ teaspoon black pepper. Whisk again to thoroughly combine.

**5.** Add the whipped cottage cheese to the egg mixture and whisk until smooth.

*(recipe continues)*

• • •

**6.** Lastly, add the cooled pepper/sausage/onion mixture to the egg/cottage cheese mixture and stir to combine.

**7.** Using a ¼ cup measure, scoop the egg mixture into a standard-size muffin pan, one scoop per muffin cup. You'll have some egg mixture leftover, so you'll have to wash the muffin tin and start over to cook the remaining 4 bites. If you have two muffin tins, you can cook them at the same time on racks in the upper and lower thirds of the oven.

**8.** Pour the 10 cups of hot water into a heatproof dish that the muffin tin fits into, like a large glass Pyrex casserole dish, and set the muffin tin in the water. You want the water to come at least two-thirds up the side of the cups.

**9.** Carefully put the muffin tin sitting in the water bath into the oven (it's helpful to place the dish on a baking sheet) and bake until the center of the egg bites are set and a knife inserted into the center comes out clean, 30 to 35 minutes. If you are baking the egg bites without a water bath, they should cook within 12 to 15 minutes.

**10.** Cool slightly, then run a small offset spatula around the edges to loosen the bites and serve. The bites may be stored in an airtight container in the refrigerator for up to one week. Reheat in a microwave or air fryer for a few minutes until heated through.

I'm obsessed with smoothies—I make them all the time, as many of you may have seen in my vlogs. They're my go-to for a quick breakfast or post-workout snack. Pro tip: I love using frozen fruit instead of ice to get a more concentrated flavor, and it keeps the smoothie from getting watered down. I add protein powder for a nutrition boost, but feel free to opt out. As a chocolate-covered strawberry lover, this is an easy way to get my sweet-craving fix in the morning, while also getting closer to hitting my protein goals. Feel free to swap out the strawberries with frozen blueberries, frozen peaches, or any other frozen fruit to get that chocolate-covered fruit deliciousness!

# CHOCOLATE-COVERED STRAWBERRY SMOOTHIE

### Makes 1 smoothie

- 1 cup whole milk or milk of choice, plus more as needed
- 1 cup frozen strawberries
- ½ frozen banana
- 1 teaspoon dark cocoa powder
- 1 teaspoon peanut butter
- 1 scoop chocolate protein powder (optional)
- 1 whole fresh strawberry, for garnish

**1.** In a high-speed blender, combine the milk, strawberries, banana, cocoa powder, peanut butter, and, if using, the protein powder.

**2.** Run the blender on high until the mixture is completely smooth, 1 to 2 minutes. Add extra milk as needed to reach your desired consistency and top with a strawberry.

If there's one thing about me, I'm getting the chia pudding if it's on the menu. I eat this simple morning meal on the regular because it's so easy to prep, and as a girl with PCOS (polycystic ovary syndrome), I find it's a great lower-carb breakfast with lots of fiber. I prep four servings at once, which easily carry me through the week. I especially like how customizable the pudding base is so I don't get bored with the same flavors. Besides different fresh fruits, you can mix in cocoa or matcha powder, protein powder, nuts, or even a spoonful of Nutella. I am excited when I wake up knowing I have my chia seed pudding, and it leaves me feeling so energized, and like a "hot girl" ready to take on her day!

# HOT GIRL COCONUT CHIA PUDDING

### Makes 4 cups

- 2 (13.5-ounce) cans (about 4 cups) coconut milk
- 1 cup chia seeds
- 4 tablespoons maple syrup
- 1 teaspoon pure vanilla extract
- ¼ cup or more of your favorite fresh fruits such as berries, sliced bananas, or mango
- Sweetened or unsweetened coconut flakes, for garnish

**1.** Into each of four 12-ounce, preferably lidded, containers or jars (or bigger), add 1 cup coconut milk, ¼ cup chia seeds, 1 tablespoon maple syrup, and ¼ teaspoon vanilla. Stir to combine.

**2.** Cover with a lid or plastic wrap and put the containers in the fridge to set overnight.

**3.** When ready to serve, top with your favorite fresh fruit and garnish with coconut flakes. The puddings will keep in the refrigerator for up to 5 days. Add milk as needed to thin to your desired consistency.

### LET'S GET CREATIVE!

Swap out the coconut milk in the chia pudding for any milk, dairy or non, you like.

You can also replace the maple syrup with other sweeteners such as honey or agave.

Toppings and mix-ins are where you can really get imaginative . . . think nut butters, granolas, jams.

If you don't have lidded jars or containers, use wineglasses or even mugs.

Inspired by my Out-of-This-World Galaxy Brownies (page 105), these oats have that same rich, chocolatey brownie-like flavor but with a healthier twist. Packed with fiber and nutrients, this make-ahead meal will keep you fueled all day. As with my Hot Girl Coconut Chia Pudding (page 48), I like to prep this recipe Sunday so I'm set for the week. If you don't want to wait overnight, try these oats cooked (see Let's Get Creative!). I almost like them better that way, but I'll let you be the judge.

# GALAXY BROWNIE OVERNIGHT OATS

### *Makes 4 containers*

- 4 cups dairy or nondairy milk of choice
- ¼ cup dark cocoa powder
- ¼ cup maple syrup or sweetener of choice
- ½ teaspoon pure vanilla extract
- Kosher salt
- 2 cups quick-cooking or old-fashioned oats
- ¼ cup chia seeds
- Cosmic brownie sprinkles or rainbow candy-coated chocolate chips (see page 105)

**1.** In a medium bowl, whisk together the milk, cocoa powder, maple syrup, vanilla, and a pinch of salt until smooth. Stir in the oats and chia seeds and divide the mixture evenly between four 12-ounce or larger lidded jars or containers.

**2.** Cover and refrigerate overnight.

**3.** Before serving, garnish with sprinkles for a fun touch. Enjoy cold. The overnight oats will keep in the refrigerator for up to 5 days. Stir in milk as needed to thin to your desired consistency before eating.

### LET'S GET CREATIVE!

Give these oats your own flair by adding cut-up fresh fruit such as bananas or strawberries, chopped nuts, or even a spoonful of peanut butter.

If you prefer your oats warm, instead of refrigerating, heat them in the microwave for 1 minute 30 seconds to 2 minutes, then stir before eating. Add more milk, if needed, to reach your desired consistency.

My favorite Parsons family holiday tradition is a Taco Bell breakfast. The first time I went to Minnesota to meet Cal's family, I remember waking up Christmas morning to his dad asking what I wanted from Taco Bell. I was so confused because I didn't even know Taco Bell had breakfast. I'm a Crunch Wrap girl, so obviously I sprang for their Breakfast Crunch Wrap and my life was forever changed. You'll see I call for raw tortillas, which aren't required, but up the tortilla game significantly. Since they aren't precooked like most run-of-the-mill store-bought tortillas, raw tortillas are as close to homemade as you'll get (think of precooked tortillas like grocery store bagged bread and raw tortillas like bakery bread). I also like to make these breakfast wraps in advance and reheat them.

# BACONY CHEESY EGGY CRUNCHY BREAKFAST WRAP

### Serves 4

- 12 ounces (about 12 slices) sliced pork bacon
- 2 cups (about 6 ounces) frozen shredded hash browns
- 6 large eggs
- ½ teaspoon garlic powder
- ½ teaspoon onion powder
- ¼ teaspoon kosher salt, plus more as needed
- Freshly ground black pepper
- 4 raw or precooked 10-inch flour tortillas
- 2 cups (8 ounces) shredded Mexican cheese
- 4 (4- to 6-inch) crispy tostadas
- Sweet Sriracha Mayo (page 24), salsa, hot sauce, and/or sour cream, for serving

**1.** In a large, cold nonstick skillet, lay some bacon strips in a single layer, making sure they do not overlap (cook the bacon in smaller batches if necessary). Turn the heat to medium and cook the bacon until browned and almost crispy, using tongs to turn it so both sides cook evenly (it'll crisp up a little more as it cools), 5 to 7 minutes. Transfer the cooked bacon to a paper towel-lined plate. Transfer the bacon fat from the skillet to a heatproof container (reserve it to use with the hash browns) before cooking a new batch. Repeat with the rest of the bacon until all the bacon is cooked. When the bacon is cool, cut it into 1-inch pieces.

**2.** Add any remaining fat to the reserved fat, and, using a paper towel, wipe out the skillet and place it over medium heat. Add the hash browns, season with a few pinches of salt, and cook for 3 minutes, stirring occasionally. After the hash browns are defrosted and become soft, add 2 tablespoons of the bacon fat and toss to coat. Spread out the hash browns in a single layer and allow them to cook, undisturbed, until they start to crisp up on the bottom, about 4 minutes. Using a spatula, turn the hash browns and cook until they crisp up on the other side, another 4 minutes or so. Place the hash browns on a plate and set aside.

*(recipe continues)*

••• 

**3.** Next, crack the eggs into a medium bowl and whisk until the yolks and whites are combined. Add the garlic powder, onion powder, the ¼ teaspoon salt, and a few pinches of pepper and whisk again until fully combined. Place 2 tablespoons of the reserved bacon fat into the skillet you just used for the hash browns and heat over medium heat, swirling the grease around to coat the pan.

**4.** Pour the eggs into the middle of the pan, and, using a rubber spatula, slowly stir the eggs, scraping the mixture so it doesn't stick. As large, soft curds start to form, reduce the heat to low and slowly flip the eggs to preserve the curds. As soon as all the liquid egg is cooked, transfer the scrambled eggs to a bowl or plate.

**5.** If using raw tortillas, heat the skillet over high heat and warm the tortillas for about 30 seconds on each side. Transfer the warmed tortillas to a baking sheet, where you will fill them.

**6.** Spread the tortillas out flat on your baking sheet or the counter/workspace, and divide the fillings evenly into the center of each one, starting with the cheese, then bacon, then eggs, and finally the crunchy hash browns and top with a tostada. Starting with one side, fold the tortilla in toward the center, then pleat the tortilla to create a second fold, and repeat this process until the entire tortilla is wrapped up. You should have 5 to 6 folds. Flip the folded tortilla wrap over so the folds are face down. Repeat this until all the tortillas, fillings, and tostadas are used.

**7.** Heat your skillet over medium, and very carefully transfer a folded wrap to the pan, folded side down, and cook the wrap until the tortilla just starts to brown, about four minutes. Flip it over and repeat on the other side. If you can fit more than one wrap in the pan at once, do! Repeat the process with the remaining wraps until they are all cooked.

**8.** Serve the wraps warm with sriracha mayo, salsa, hot sauce, and/or sour cream. Cooked breakfast wraps may be wrapped in plastic wrap or foil and stored in the refrigerator for up to 2 days. To reheat, warm the wrap in a skillet over medium heat until it starts to crisp up, then flip it and place a lid on the skillet, lower the heat, and continue to cook until the wrap is heated through.

### LET'S USE THE OVEN

If you want to save time making these breakfast wraps, consider baking your bacon and hash browns instead of frying them. Arrange 2 racks in the top and bottom thirds of the oven and preheat it to 400°F. For the bacon: Line a rimmed baking sheet with foil. If you have a wire rack that fits on your baking sheet, use it. If not, you can cook the bacon just fine without one.

Spread the bacon out in a single layer on the rack or the pan, making sure it doesn't overlap.

Bake on the upper rack until the bacon is crispy or to your desired doneness, about 15 minutes. Using tongs or a fork, transfer the bacon to a paper towel–lined plate and use as directed in the recipe.

For the hash browns: Put them in a bowl and toss with 2 tablespoons extra-virgin olive oil and sprinkle with salt and pepper and toss to coat. Spread the hash browns out evenly on a baking sheet and press down. Bake on the lower rack until the top is golden brown and crispy, then flip, and continue to bake until both sides are golden brown and crispy, about 40 minutes total.

I am obsessed with decorating, designing, and planning. As a little girl, I always dreamed of my own house, and in it, I imagined myself hosting. My dreams have come true, and during any holiday, special event, or even a random Tuesday, you'll pretty much always find my friends and family over at my house celebrating and eating. My love language is food. I adore serving people—the more, the better. I like having generous spreads (see my favorite menus for hosting on page 64), and I'm big on dishes that can be made completely ahead so I can spend more time with my guests. Hosting, however, does not need to be for a crowd. I'll use any excuse to throw a party, no matter what the occasion. I recently threw Cal a first-Packers'-game-of-the-season party, all for just him and me. There's no wrong occasion for fun appetizers, drinks, and good company!

Cal's Salted Caramel Cold Foam Espresso Martini   60

Strawberry Lemonade Tequila Batch Cocktail   63

Air Fryer Miso-Butter–Glazed Shishito Peppers   65

Caramelized Onion Dip   67

Bacon Cheese Dip with Fried Pita Bread   68

Party-Pleaser Goat Cheese–Stuffed Dates   71

Cheesy Jalapeño Poppers   72

Spicy Salmon and Avocado on Crispy Rice   73

Smashed Parmesan-Crusted Brussels Sprouts   76

Crispy Tempura Green Beans with Garlic Aioli   79

Angel and Deviled Eggs   80

Miso Honey–Glazed Sea Bass Cups   83

Super-Easy Slow Cooker Meatballs   85

Suz's Cornflake Potato Casserole   87

Best-Ever Garlic Butter Rolls   89

Fried Crab Rangoons with Sweet Chili Sauce   91

Japanese Air-Fried Chicken Bites   92

Garlic Parmesan Chicken Wings   95

Sweetest Strawberry Butter Cake Bars   97

World's Best Cakey Chocolate Chip Cookies   103

Out-of-This-World Galaxy Brownies   105

Brown Butter Sugar Cookies   109

Ooey Gooey Chocolate Caramel Candy Bars   111

This sweet and creamy espresso martini is the perfect decadent cocktail. The salted caramel cold foam adds a luxurious touch that elevates this classic drink to a new level. (Also, you can make just the cold foam and use it as a delicious addition to your morning coffee.) This is my husband Cal's recipe—he's a cocktail connoisseur! It's one of my favorite Cocktails with Cal original recipes. If you don't have an espresso machine, consider getting two take-out espressos for this recipe. Instant espresso works well in a pinch, too. If you are grinding your espresso at home, garnishing with three espresso beans is said to bring good luck—so why not!

# CAL'S SALTED CARAMEL COLD FOAM ESPRESSO MARTINI

## Makes 2 drinks

- ¼ cup (2 ounces) brewed medium roast espresso
- ¼ cup (2 ounces) coffee liqueur such as Mr. Black Cold Brew Coffee Liqueur
- ¼ cup (2 ounces) vodka
- 1 tablespoon Simple Syrup (recipe follows)
- 2 tablespoons heavy cream, divided
- 1 tablespoon caramel sauce or syrup
- Kosher salt
- 6 espresso beans, for garnish (optional)

**1.** To a cocktail shaker filled with ice, combine the espresso, coffee liqueur, vodka, Simple Syrup, and 1 tablespoon of the cream. Shake vigorously until the shaker is cold and frosty. Strain the mixture evenly into 2 coupe or martini glasses.

**2.** In a small container with a lid, such as a glass jar, combine the remaining tablespoon of cream, the caramel sauce, and a pinch of salt. Shake vigorously for 2 to 3 minutes, until the mixture becomes foamy. Spoon the salted caramel cold foam over each martini, creating an even layer.

**3.** To serve, garnish each drink with 3 espresso beans, if desired, for a bit of luck.

### LET'S GET MAKING SIMPLE SYRUP!

Simple syrup is a classic sweetener for almost any cocktail because it's purely liquid and distributes evenly through a drink (as opposed to dumping in a spoonful of sugar that doesn't dissolve). To make the simple syrup: In a saucepan over medium-high heat, combine equal parts sugar and water (e.g., 1 cup granulated sugar and 1 cup water) and bring the mixture to a boil, stirring until the sugar has dissolved, then remove the pan from the heat and let the syrup cool before using. Store in a jar or lidded container in the refrigerator for up to 1 month. Since you just need about a tablespoon of syrup for the martini recipe above, you can also put 2 tablespoons water and 2 tablespoons sugar in the microwave on high and cook until the sugar melts, about 1 minute. You'll have a little more syrup than you need, but the extra allows for any spillage or evaporation.

My husband, Cal, and I had so much fun concocting this batch cocktail together (remember, I mentioned he's a cocktail connoisseur). We wanted a drink perfect for warm days spent with friends, and this cocktail captures that vibe perfectly! The bright, refreshing flavors of lemon and strawberry make it a real crowd-pleaser. For those who prefer a nonalcoholic option, skip the tequila and you'll have a delicious strawberry lemonade mocktail. Or, if you're more of a vodka girl like me, feel free to switch out the liquor for one of your preference. Add a splash of sparkling water for an extra refreshing spritz and enjoy a sip of sunshine!

# STRAWBERRY LEMONADE TEQUILA BATCH COCKTAIL

### Makes 6 to 8 cocktails

- 16 ounces fresh or frozen hulled strawberries, coarsely chopped (about 3 cups), plus 6 to 8 strawberry slices, for garnish (optional)
- 1 cup water, divided
- ½ cup freshly squeezed lemon juice
- ½ cup (4 ounces) tequila of choice
- ¼ cup (2 ounces) Simple Syrup (page 60)
- 2 to 3 cups ice, for serving
- 6 to 8 lemon slices, for garnish
- 2 to 3 stems fresh mint leaves, for garnish
- 8 to 12 ounces sparkling water or club soda, for serving (optional)

**1.** In a medium saucepan over low heat, combine the chopped strawberries and ½ cup of water (if you are using frozen strawberries, omit the water), mashing and stirring occasionally until the berries are completely softened, about 15 minutes. Using a fine-mesh strainer, push the mixture through into a large pitcher to remove any solids. Let the mixture cool.

**2.** In the large pitcher with the cooled strawberry mixture, add the remaining ½ cup of water, the lemon juice, tequila, and syrup. Stir well and taste, adding more syrup or water based on your taste preference. Chill until ready to serve.

**3.** When ready to serve, fill glasses half full with the ice and then pour in the lemonade. Garnish with a lemon slice, fresh mint, and, if using, a strawberry slice. For a bubbly version, top with a splash of sparkling water or club soda. The batched cocktail can be prepared up to 12 hours in advance and refrigerated until ready to serve.

## Game-Changing Game Day Snacks

My go-to make-ahead recipes:

Caramelized Onion Dip   67

Cheesy Jalapeño Poppers   72

Super-Easy Slow Cooker Meatballs   85

Garlic Parmesan Chicken Wings   95

Out-of-This-World Galaxy Brownies   105

Brown Butter Sugar Cookies   109

## A Special Birthday Menu

Dishes to make your birthday king or queen feel special:

Air Fryer Miso-Butter-Glazed Shishito Peppers   65

Party-Pleaser Goat Cheese–Stuffed Dates   71

Spicy Salmon and Avocado on Crispy Rice   73

Miso Honey-Glazed Sea Bass Cups   83

Fried Crab Rangoons with Sweet Chili Sauce   91

Sweetest Strawberry Butter Cake Bars   97

## Holiday Favorites

My all-time favorites for a classic Cruz holiday:

Smashed Parmesan-Crusted Brussels Sprouts   76

Crispy Tempura Green Beans with Garlic Aioli   79

Angel and Deviled Eggs   80

Suz's Cornflake Potato Casserole   87

Best-Ever Garlic Butter Rolls   89

World's Best Cakey Chocolate Chip Cookies   103

## Girl's Night Menu

Drinks, dips, fried bites, and a sweet treat to hit all the notes for the girls:

Cal's Salted Caramel Cold Foam Espresso Martini   60

Strawberry Lemonade Tequila Batch Cocktail   63

Bacon Cheese Dip with Fried Pita Bread   68

Party-Pleaser Goat Cheese–Stuffed Dates   71

Japanese Air-Fried Chicken Bites   92

Ooey Gooey Chocolate Caramel Candy Bars   111

Whenever shishito pepper season comes around, you can often find me doing a little happy dance in the grocery store produce section. They're one of my favorite vegetables, and I believe they are severely underrated. Eating shishito peppers can be like a fun game of roulette—about one in every ten packs a spicy punch! As simple as it is, the rich, savory miso-butter glaze I use here has a lot of depth—you'll want to drizzle it on everything. Think shrimp, other roasted veggies, or even a biscuit (see page 137). Or, instead of drizzling the glaze *over* the peppers, you can put it in a small bowl and use it as a dip. I like this dish as a side or for a super-easy brunch; it works well paired with my Croissant Breakfast Bake (page 139), too. I also love just snacking on these sweet-and-sometimes-spicy chiles. Try it out and see how many hot ones you get!

# AIR FRYER MISO-BUTTER-GLAZED SHISHITO PEPPERS

### Serves 4

- 1 tablespoon extra-virgin olive oil
- 8 ounces fresh shishito peppers
- ¼ teaspoon kosher salt, plus more for seasoning
- 3 tablespoons unsalted butter
- 2 tablespoons white miso paste
- 2 tablespoons honey
- 1 tablespoon water

1. Preheat your air fryer to 375°F.

2. In a medium bowl, drizzle the olive oil over the peppers, sprinkle with 2 pinches of salt, and toss to coat.

3. In a saucepan over medium-low heat, melt the butter. Whisk in the miso, honey, water, and the ¼ teaspoon of salt. Whisk until the mixture begins to boil, then turn off the heat. Taste the glaze and add more salt as needed depending on the saltiness of your miso. Set aside.

4. Cook your shishitos in the air fryer until slightly charred and blistered, 6 to 8 minutes.

5. To serve, using tongs or a fork, transfer the cooked shishitos to a platter and drizzle with the miso-butter glaze. The peppers are best eaten right away.

#### Remi's Recommendations

If you don't have an air fryer, you can blister your peppers on the stovetop in a skillet over high heat. Cook until they start to char on one side, 3 to 4 minutes, then shake the pan or flip using tongs, and continue to cook on the other side until charred, then drizzle with glaze as directed above.

LET'S GET HOSTING

If I'm throwing a party, I can guarantee this dip will be there because it's a huge hit with my girlfriends. I've always loved onion dip, and after years of making it with powdered onion packets, I took the time to make it from scratch, and I swear I'll never look back. Prepare yourself: Properly caramelized onions take quite a while to cook, but it is SO worth it! When you cut the onions, you want to slice them as thinly as possible. It'll seem like *a lot* of onion because *it is* a lot of onion. In my opinion, this dip pairs well with pretty much anything: ruffled potato chips, kettle chips, fried pita—it even makes raw vegetables taste good!

# CARAMELIZED ONION DIP

### *Makes about 1 quart dip*

- 4 tablespoons (½ stick) unsalted butter
- 5 large sweet onions, sliced as thinly as possible
- Kosher salt
- Freshly ground black pepper
- 1 cup (8 ounces) cream cheese, softened
- 1 cup (8 ounces) sour cream
- 2 tablespoons ranch seasoning
- 1 tablespoon chopped fresh dill (optional)
- 1 tablespoon chopped fresh chives (optional)
- Ruffled potato chips, for serving

### Remi's Recommendations

For this recipe, the thinner your onions are, the better, because they'll cook faster. You want them almost paper thin. If you have one, I recommend using a mandoline on the thinnest setting to cut the onions.

**1.** In a 12-inch skillet (or larger) over medium-low heat, melt the butter. Add the onions, stir to coat with the butter, and sprinkle with a few generous pinches of salt and pepper. Cook, stirring intermittently, until the onions are soft, golden, and caramelized, 45 to 90 minutes. I know this is a huge time span, but many factors can affect how long the onions take to caramelize. You don't want to cut the cooking time short and you also don't want the onions to get mushy. Just look for the warm golden color and you'll be set. If the pan seems dry at any time, add 1 or 2 tablespoons of water. You may need to do this more than once. Remove the caramelized onions from the heat and transfer them to a bowl or plate to cool.

**2.** Meanwhile, in a large bowl, combine the cream cheese, sour cream, and ranch seasoning and whisk until smooth (this is a Midwest dream, lol). Gently fold in the cooled caramelized onions, reserving some for garnish. You may want to start slowly, adding about a cup, then adding the rest in ¼-cup increments until you reach your desired consistency. If you add them all, like I do, you'll get a VERY oniony dip. It's almost like onions are bound together by the cream cheese/sour cream mixture. If you like a creamier dip, add more cream cheese and sour cream, *or* hold back some of the onions and use them to top a burger (try my BBB, page 131), or add extra onions to my Caramelized Onion Chicken (page 215). What can I say? I love caramelized onions.

**3.** For a brighter dip, stir in the dill and chives. Top with the reserved caramelized onions and serve with ruffled potato chips. To store, refrigerate the dip in an airtight container for up to 4 days.

LET'S GET HOSTING

This addictive dip has become my ultimate appetizer when hosting. I cook the bacon in the oven, making it pretty simple to throw together, and cleanup is much easier with no messy frying pan to wash. This dip has cheesy, salty, creamy comfort-food vibes, giving it a game-day feel. When I first made this dip for my best friends Lauren and Mia, they couldn't get over how much they loved it. Now I make sure to have it ready for any girls' night and bring it to almost every party. The fried pita bread was inspired by a restaurant that originated in my hometown called Slater's 50/50. The pita is so simple, but it's such an elevated option compared to a bowl of chips.

# BACON CHEESE DIP WITH FRIED PITA BREAD

## Serves 8 to 10

**FOR THE DIP**

- 16 ounces (about 16 strips) sliced pork bacon
- 1½ cups (12 ounces) sour cream
- 1 cup (8 ounces) cream cheese, softened
- 1 tablespoon garlic powder
- 1 tablespoon onion powder
- 1 teaspoon paprika
- ½ teaspoon kosher salt
- ¼ teaspoon freshly ground black pepper
- 2 cups (8 ounces) shredded cheddar cheese
- 3 green onions (white and green parts), chopped

**FOR THE FRIED PITA**

- 1 quart vegetable oil or other high-heat neutral oil, for frying
- 6 large pitas (I like Papa Pita's white pitas), each cut into 6 triangles
- Flaky salt, for sprinkling

**1.** Arrange 2 oven racks in the upper and lower thirds of your oven. Preheat the oven to 400°F.

**2.** Make the dip: Line 2 rimmed baking sheets with foil and arrange the bacon strips in a single layer on each sheet, dividing the bacon between the two. Bake until the bacon starts to turn crispy, 15 to 20 minutes. Transfer the bacon to a paper towel–lined plate to cool, then roughly chop it and set aside.

**3.** In a large mixing bowl, combine the sour cream and cream cheese, stirring until well combined.

**4.** Add the garlic powder, onion powder, paprika, salt, and pepper and stir to combine. Stir in the cheddar cheese, green onions, and chopped bacon minus a couple teaspoons of each (set these aside to use as garnish). Transfer the dip to a 7 x 9-inch baking dish (or something comparable like an 8-inch round or square oven-safe dish) and bake until the cheese has melted and the dip is heated through, about 25 minutes. While the dip bakes, fry the pitas.

**5.** Make the pitas: In a 2- or 3-quart pot with a candy thermometer, over high heat, bring the oil to 350°F (your oil should be 1 to 1½ inches deep, see page 23 for more on frying). Working in small batches, using tongs or a small spider, lower the pitas into the oil and fry until golden brown, about 30 seconds. If you can, try to turn the pitas after 15 seconds to cook evenly on both sides. Be careful, they cook quickly! The pitas will be slightly crisped on the outside and still soft inside. If you want crispier pita chips and your pitas have pockets, you can slice the pockets apart for a single-layer chip. Fry until crispy and golden, about 15 seconds (they are half the pita so they cook in about half the time!). Transfer the fried pita chips to a paper towel-lined plate and sprinkle with flaky salt.

**6.** Serve the dip warm topped with the reserved cheese, bacon, and green onions and a side of warm pita chips. And there you have it! So good. To store, refrigerate the dip in an airtight container for up to 4 days.

### Remi's Recommendations

You can easily make this dip ahead for a stress-free celebration or an easy girls' night snack. You have two options: 1) Make the dip but don't bake it (you can make this up to 2 days in advance). Instead, cover it with foil and refrigerate. One hour before serving the dip, remove it from the fridge and bring it to room temperature for 30 minutes before heating. 2) You can cook the dip and reheat it in a microwave-safe dish at 50 percent power in 30 second intervals until warmed through. (If you heat it on high, the cheese may separate.) You can also reheat it, covered, in a 350°F oven until it's warmed through.

Honestly, bacon-wrapped anything always sounds delicious, but these savory-sweet bacon-wrapped dates truly rank as a family favorite. Cal could finish off a plate of these by himself! The tanginess of the goat cheese is perfectly balanced by the sweetness of the dates, all wrapped in crispy, decadent bacon. If you're not a huge fan of goat cheese, you could try subbing in feta or blue cheese. With minimal prep and a festive presentation, this recipe checks all the boxes for a perfect girls' night bite.

# PARTY-PLEASER GOAT CHEESE-STUFFED DATES

### *Makes 32 date bites*

- 1 (12-ounce) package (about 32) medium pitted Medjool dates
- 1 (8-ounce) log goat cheese
- 16 ounces (about 16 strips) sliced pork bacon, cut in half, which should yield 3- to 4-inch pieces
- Hot Honey (page 24) or store-bought, for serving (optional)
- Flaky salt, for serving

1. Preheat the oven to 400°F. Line a baking sheet with parchment paper and set aside.

2. Spread each date open at the slit and add a teaspoonful of goat cheese to the center, then press it closed.

3. Wrap each goat cheese-stuffed date with a piece of the trimmed bacon, then pierce the bacon with a toothpick to secure.

4. Arrange the stuffed dates on the prepared baking sheet, with the toothpicks all lying to the same side. Bake for 10 minutes, then turn all the toothpicks so they are all facing the other way, essentially turning each date so it bakes on the other side and prevents the bottom from burning.

5. Bake until the bacon is crispy, about another 10 minutes. Check the bottoms of the dates after about 7 minutes to make sure they aren't burning. If they are, flip the dates again.

6. Remove from the oven and serve as is, or, if using, drizzle with the honey and a sprinkle of flaky salt. The dates are best eaten warm, when the bacon is crispy. You may make the dates one day ahead and store them in the refrigerator. To serve, reheat the dates in a 350°F oven until warmed through, 5 to 8 minutes.

### Remi's Recommendations

When cutting the bacon in half for this recipe, I like to cut straight through the packaging with a sharp kitchen knife. This keeps the bacon together when slicing. Another option is to use kitchen shears.

I never liked jalapeños until I met these poppers, which combine some of the best things life offers—cheese, cream cheese, and bacon. They're creamy and cheesy and obvi perfect for game day (Cal's family is a BIG football family). I always get excited to make them because they are a no-brainer. You can prep them up to a day ahead, cover them tightly in the fridge, and cook them right before your guests arrive. I can't believe I've been missing out on this deliciousness for thirty years.

# CHEESY JALAPEÑO POPPERS

### Makes 16 to 20 poppers

- 1 cup (8 ounces) cream cheese, softened
- 1 teaspoon garlic powder
- 1 teaspoon onion powder
- 1 teaspoon kosher salt
- ¼ teaspoon freshly ground black pepper
- ¾ cup shredded cheddar cheese
- 8 to 10 fresh medium jalapeños, halved and seeded
- 10 ounces (about 10 slices) sliced pork bacon, cut in half crosswise
- Granulated sugar
- 1 to 2 tablespoons chopped chives, for garnish

**1.** Preheat the oven to 400°F. Line a baking sheet with parchment paper. Set aside.

**2.** In a medium bowl, stir together the cream cheese, garlic powder, onion powder, salt, and pepper until well combined. Add the cheddar cheese and stir again until well combined.

**3.** Using a tablespoon, fill the jalapeño halves with the cheese mixture, filling each one flush with the edges.

**4.** Wrap a ½ slice of bacon around each cheese-filled jalapeño, using a toothpick if needed to secure the bacon. The bacon stretches some, so you should be able to wrap it around about 1½ times so the seam/end of the bacon lands around the back of the pepper. Place the peppers about an inch apart, cheese side up, on the prepared baking sheet. Sprinkle with a light dusting of sugar before baking. Bake until the peppers have softened and the cheese just starts to turn slightly golden, about 35 minutes.

**5.** Serve warm garnished with the chives. The poppers may be prepped ahead and stored covered in the refrigerator for up to 1 day, then bake as directed. Baked poppers may be stored in the refrigerator for up to 3 days and reheated in a 350°F oven until warmed through, 8 to 10 minutes.

If I'm out to dinner and there's crispy rice on the menu, I guarantee I'm ordering it. It's so trendy right now. You'll find it in restaurants topped with many different types of fish or vegetables. In this particular version I use salmon, which is eaten raw, so be sure you are getting sushi-grade fish. Ask your fishmonger or look for frozen salmon labeled sushi- or sashimi-grade. I think it's fun to get creative with this dish because it's easy to customize. You can swap toppings and even change the shape of the rice before frying; instead of cutting it into squares, sometimes I use a cookie cutter to make circles or hearts. Pro tip: Dust the cookie cutters with cornstarch first so the rice doesn't stick. You can also use a knife to freeform it and get really inventive for your next party!

# SPICY SALMON AND AVOCADO ON CRISPY RICE

*Makes 16 square salmon bites*

### FOR THE SUSHI RICE

- 2 cups uncooked sushi rice
- 2 cups water
- 1 tablespoon rice vinegar
- 2 teaspoons granulated sugar
- 1 teaspoon kosher salt

### FOR THE SALMON

- 2 tablespoons Kewpie mayonnaise
- 1 tablespoon sriracha
- 1 tablespoon soy sauce
- 1 green onion, minced, white and green parts separated
- 8 ounces skinless sushi-grade salmon fillet, finely diced
- 1/3 to 2/3 cup vegetable oil or other high-heat neutral oil, for frying
- 1 avocado, thinly cut into 16 slices
- 2 to 3 tablespoons eel sauce, for drizzling (optional)
- 1 to 2 tablespoons black or white sesame seeds (I like to use a combo!)

1. Make the sushi rice: In a fine-mesh strainer, rinse the rice with cold water until the water runs clear. Drain the rice and put it in a medium pot with a lid. Add the water. Bring to a boil over medium-high heat and then reduce the heat to low, cover, and let the rice cook until it's tender to the bite, about 15 minutes, or as instructed on the rice package.

2. Remove the cooked rice from the heat and let it stand, covered, for 10 minutes.

3. In a small bowl, combine the rice vinegar, sugar, and salt and stir until the sugar and salt have dissolved. After the rice has rested, uncover and fluff it with a fork. Sprinkle the vinegar mixture over the rice and toss to coat.

4. In an 8 x 8-inch square pan or casserole dish, spoon in the cooled, cooked sushi rice, spreading it as evenly as possible. Using the back of a spatula, press the rice into an even layer. Cover the dish with plastic wrap and refrigerate for at least 6 hours, or overnight.

5. Prepare the salmon: In a medium bowl, stir together the mayonnaise, sriracha, soy sauce, and the white parts of the green onion. Add the salmon and gently toss to coat. Cover and refrigerate until you are ready to assemble the rice squares.

*(recipe continues)*

●●●

**6.** Fry the rice squares: Cut the chilled rice into 16 equal squares (they will be 2 x 2 inches). Using a spatula, remove the rice squares from the pan or dish and put them on a plate for easy access while you are frying.

**7.** Heat ⅓ cup of oil in a large 12-inch skillet over high heat until it shimmers. You want to ensure the oil is hot so the rice cooks quickly. You can test the oil by lowering a small cube of bread into the oil. If it sizzles and bubbles and turns golden in under a minute, the oil is hot enough. If not, wait and repeat the process with a new cube of bread until the oil is hot.

**8.** Using a slotted spatula if you have one (otherwise, a regular one works), lower the rice squares into the hot oil, allowing for space around each rice square. You don't want them to touch. (You will likely need to fry the rice squares in two batches.) Fry the rice squares in the oil until the bottoms turn a light golden color, 2 to 3 minutes, then, using the spatula, turn them to fry on the second side and continue to cook until the rice turns a light golden color, another 2 to 3 minutes. You can remove one square and test it for doneness by cutting off a small slice and biting into it. You want the rice crispy on the outside yet soft on the inside. If you cook the squares too long, they can become hard and crunchy. We are going for lightly crispy. When they are finished cooking, transfer the golden rice squares to a paper towel-lined plate.

**9.** Repeat the frying process until all the squares are cooked, adding more oil as needed.

**10.** When you are ready to serve the bites, assemble the cooked rice squares on a serving platter. Top each square with a slice of avocado and then about 1 tablespoon of the salmon mixture. Drizzle with the eel sauce, if using, and sprinkle with the sesame seeds. Garnish with the green parts of the green onion. The crispy rice bites are best eaten right away.

When I eat out, one of my go-to appetizers is Brussels sprouts because sometimes I just need more vegetables in my life. At home, I also serve Brussels as an appetizer, or as a side dish, or even a salad topper. These sprouts have a wonderfully autumnal feel, and they make a great side for Thanksgiving dinner—but really, they are enjoyable any time of the year!

# SMASHED PARMESAN-CRUSTED BRUSSELS SPROUTS

### Serves 4 to 6

- 2 tablespoons extra-virgin olive oil, plus more for greasing the pan
- ¼ teaspoon kosher salt, plus more for seasoning
- 1½ pounds whole medium Brussels sprouts, stems lightly trimmed and any exterior wilted leaves removed
- ½ cup panko breadcrumbs
- ½ cup grated Parmesan cheese
- 1 teaspoon chicken bouillon powder
- 1 teaspoon Italian seasoning
- ½ teaspoon freshly ground black pepper
- 3 tablespoons unsalted butter, melted
- ¼ cup Sweet Sriracha Mayo (page 24), for serving (optional)

**1.** Preheat the oven to 425°F. Liberally grease a baking sheet with olive oil and set aside.

**2.** Put a medium pot half filled with water over medium heat, add the ¼ teaspoon of salt, and bring the water to a boil. Add the Brussels sprouts and cook until they are fork-tender, about 12 minutes. Drain the sprouts and dry them well with paper towels. Transfer them to the greased baking sheet and let them cool enough so you can handle them without hurting your hands.

**3.** While the sprouts are cooling, in a small bowl, stir together the panko, Parmesan, chicken bouillon, Italian seasoning, and pepper. Add the melted butter and stir again to combine. Set aside.

**4.** Drizzle the somewhat cooled sprouts with the 2 tablespoons of olive oil and, using your hands, gently toss to coat. Using the bottom of a coffee mug or glass cup, gently press down on one sprout at a time to smash them directly on the baking sheet. The flatter they are, the crispier they get. Sprinkle the sprouts with a pinch of salt.

**5.** Bake the sprouts until they start to turn ever-so-slightly brown on the bottoms, about 15 minutes. Using a spatula, gently flip the sprouts and bake for another 5 minutes. Pull the sprouts from the oven and sprinkle each one with the panko/Parmesan mixture, dividing it evenly between the sprouts. Reduce the oven temperature to 400°F and bake until the panko turns golden and the cheese melts, another 10 minutes or so.

**6.** Remove from the oven and serve warm with the sriracha mayo if desired. The sprouts are best eaten right away.

I will always be a green bean girl. Whether fried, steamed, tempura-style, sauteed, or casseroled—I will always be ordering the green beans off any menu. These beans are a fun twist on a french fry, but better because the tempura batter is lighter, airier, and crispier than a traditional deep-fry coating.

# CRISPY TEMPURA GREEN BEANS WITH GARLIC AIOLI

*Serves 6 to 8 as an appetizer*

**FOR THE GARLIC AIOLI**

- ¾ cup Kewpie mayonnaise
- 2 small garlic cloves, minced or grated
- 2 teaspoons freshly squeezed lemon juice
- 1 teaspoon mirin
- ½ teaspoon kosher salt
- ¼ teaspoon freshly ground black pepper

**FOR THE BATTER**

- 1¾ cups all-purpose flour, divided
- ½ teaspoon baking soda
- ½ teaspoon kosher salt, plus more for seasoning
- 1½ cups club soda or sparkling water
- ½ cup ice
- 1 quart vegetable oil or other high-heat neutral oil, for frying
- 1 pound green beans (about 4 cups), trimmed (I like to buy the pre-trimmed ones in a bag!)
- Flaky salt, for serving

**1.** Make the garlic aioli: In a small bowl, stir together the mayonnaise, garlic, lemon juice, mirin, salt, and pepper until well combined. Set aside.

**2.** Make the batter: In a large mixing bowl, whisk together 1 cup of flour, the baking soda, and salt. Pour in the club soda and whisk again until the batter is smooth with no clumps. Add ½ cup of ice and ½ cup more of flour, and, using a spoon, stir several times, leaving the mixture slightly clumpy, which will create delicious extra bits when frying.

**3.** Fry the green beans: In a large skillet with a candy thermometer, heat the oil to 350°F (see page 23 if you don't have a thermometer and for more on frying). Line a plate with paper towels and set aside.

**4.** Meanwhile, in a medium bowl, sprinkle the remaining ¼ cup of flour over the green beans and toss to lightly coat.

**5.** Using chopsticks, tongs, or a fork, dip a green bean into the batter and let the excess run off (the batter should be quite thick; if it becomes thin and falls off the beans, add a tablespoon or two more flour to thicken it) to ensure an even coat and carefully lower the bean into the oil. Repeat the process until the pot has enough beans that they are almost touching but aren't; the beans should have room to move around. Don't overcrowd the skillet, or the oil temperature will drop, and the beans may stick together. Fry the green beans in small batches until golden brown, 1 to 2 minutes.

**6.** Transfer the cooked beans to the prepared plate and sprinkle with salt while they're still hot.

**7.** Serve the crispy green beans warm with the garlic aioli on the side for dipping. The beans are best served right away.

Ok, angel and deviled eggs aren't really that different—one just has a little more fire, and I bet you can guess which one.

# ANGEL AND DEVILED EGGS

## Makes 24 egg halves

**FOR THE ANGEL EGGS**

6 large hard-boiled eggs (page 23), peeled and cut in half lengthwise

2 tablespoons Kewpie mayonnaise

1 tablespoon pickle juice (I used bread and butter pickle juice)

1 teaspoon yellow mustard

Kosher salt

¼ cup chopped pickle, for garnish

Flaky salt, for garnish

A few fresh dill fronds, for garnish (optional)

**FOR THE DEVILED EGGS**

6 large hard-boiled eggs (page 23), peeled and cut in half lengthwise

2 tablespoons Kewpie mayonnaise

2 tablespoons sriracha or 1 teaspoon gochujang paste

Kosher salt

Gochugaru fine chili powder, for garnish

**FOR THE ANGEL EGGS**

**1.** Make the Angel Eggs: Using a spoon, scoop out the egg yolks into a large bowl, and then, using a fork, mash well.

**2.** Stir in the mayonnaise, pickle juice, mustard, and 2 to 3 pinches of salt until smooth.

**3.** Spoon the mixture into a plastic bag and cut off a small corner. Squeeze the mixture back into the egg halves and top with the chopped pickle, flaky salt, and, if using, a pinch or two of dill fronds per egg.

**4.** Refrigerate until ready to serve. Leftover eggs may be stored in an airtight container in the refrigerator for up to 3 days.

**FOR THE DEVILED EGGS**

**1.** Make the Deviled Eggs: Using a spoon, scoop out the egg yolks into a large bowl, and then, using a fork, mash well.

**2.** Stir in the mayonnaise, sriracha, and 2 to 3 pinches of salt until smooth.

**3.** Spoon the mixture into a plastic bag and cut off a small corner. Squeeze the mixture back into the egg halves and top with a sprinkling of gochugaru.

**4.** Refrigerate until ready to serve. Leftover eggs may be stored in an airtight container in the refrigerator for up to 3 days.

### Remi's Recommendations

The eggs and fillings may be prepped up to a day ahead. Keep the filling and hollowed-out eggs separate and fill within a few hours of serving. Garnish with flaky salt (for the Angel Eggs) and gochugaru fine chili powder (for the Deviled Eggs) right before serving.

Nobu is one of my favorite restaurants in LA. The food is awesome, the drinks are delicious, and the atmosphere is unbeatable. The only thing is—it's incredibly expensive and almost impossible to get a reservation. This is my take on their famed miso-marinated black cod lettuce cups that the restaurant charges $15 a pop for, so I love making them at home for a fraction of the price. The marinade is magical—it transforms fish into a sweet and tender, buttery bite. I like to use sea bass, which can be pricey (although it still works out to be cheaper than Nobu!). If the price tag seems steep, you can sub in cod or salmon. Whichever fish you use, ask your fishmonger for a center-cut fillet if possible. You want a nice, thick fish steak that will hold its shape and not fall apart. If it does, though, no worries. The lettuce cups will hold your fish if it does flake on you.

# MISO HONEY-GLAZED SEA BASS CUPS

*Serves 4 to 6 as an appetizer*

**FOR THE MARINADE**

¼ cup mirin

¼ cup sake

¼ cup white miso paste

2 tablespoons granulated sugar

2 garlic cloves, minced or grated

1½ pounds center-cut sea bass

**FOR THE TOPPING**

1 cup vegetable oil or other high-heat neutral oil for frying, plus more as needed

½ sheet phyllo dough, cut into very thin strips (if your knife isn't sharp enough, you can use kitchen shears to cut the phyllo)

**FOR THE GLAZE**

2 tablespoons unsalted butter

2 tablespoons white miso paste

**1.** Make the marinade: In a small saucepan, over medium-high heat, combine the mirin and sake and bring to a boil, cooking for about 30 seconds, or until the alcohol burns off, then reduce the heat to low.

**2.** Whisk in the miso, sugar, and garlic and continue to whisk constantly to prevent the mixture from burning. Cook over low until the marinade is smooth and well combined, 3 to 4 minutes. Set aside to allow the marinade to cool.

**3.** Meanwhile, rinse the fish, and, using paper towels, pat it dry. Cut the fish into 1-inch pieces, removing the skin if desired. Place the fish in a baking dish or wide, shallow bowl and cover with the cooled marinade, gently turning the fish to fully coat it. Cover and refrigerate the fish for at least 1 one hour and up to 3 days before cooking.

**4.** Make the topping: Just before you are ready to cook the fish, in a medium skillet over medium-high heat, pour in a ¼-inch of oil and heat until it starts to shimmer, or if you have a candy thermometer, heat the oil to 350°F (see page 23 for more on frying). Line a plate with paper

*(recipe and ingredients continue)*

2 tablespoons water

1 tablespoon Hot Honey (page 24) or store-bought

1 head baby butter lettuce, for serving (see Let's Get the Best Leaves)

Flaky salt, for serving

1 to 2 green onions (green parts only), cut on the bias, for garnish

• • •

towels and set aside. Gently slide the phyllo strips into the oil (a spider is great for this), and fry until they turn golden, about 2 minutes. They cook quickly, so keep an eye on them as they burn in seconds. Using a spider or slotted spoon, remove the crispy phyllo strips from the oil and transfer them to the prepared plate and set aside.

**5.** Next, adjust the oven rack so it's about 4 to 6 inches from the heat source and preheat the broiler. Cover a baking sheet with foil. Remove the fish from the marinade and dab it dry (you can discard the marinade), Place the pieces of fish on the prepared baking sheet (skin side down if you left the skin) and broil until the surface just begins to char; it should also flake easily when you press a fork into it, about 10 minutes.

**6.** While the fish is broiling, make the glaze: In a small saucepan, over medium heat, melt the butter, then whisk in the miso, water, and honey until smooth. Cook until it just comes to a simmer and remove from the heat.

**7.** When the fish is cooked, use a silicone brush to gently paint the glaze onto each piece of fish.

**8.** To assemble the lettuce cups, place a piece of sea bass onto each piece of lettuce, then top with crispy phyllo strips, a sprinkle of flaky salt, and garnish with the green onions. Serve and enjoy.

### LET'S GET THE BEST LEAVES!

To get ideal little lettuce cups for cradling your fish bites, peel off the large outer leaves from the lettuce head and save them for a salad or sandwich. Use the smaller leaves from the middle of the head inward for bite-size edible cups.

You guys, this is a set-it-and-forget-it recipe, which makes it absolutely perfect for parties! This sweet-and-savory holiday favorite of mine may not even seem like it needs a recipe because it's just that simple. It's three ingredients and is completely foolproof. I make these meatballs in a Crock-Pot, which I set on warm during my party to ensure they stay hot and fresh. I just put out a little bowl of toothpicks for guests to grab and enjoy!

# SUPER-EASY SLOW COOKER MEATBALLS

*Makes about 50 small meatballs*

- 1 cup grape jelly
- 1 cup of your favorite barbecue sauce
- 1 (24-ounce) bag frozen Swedish or homestyle meatballs

**1.** In a slow cooker, stir together the grape jelly and barbecue sauce until combined. Add the frozen meatballs, toss to coat with the sauce, cover, and cook until the meatballs are warmed through and the sauce becomes bubbly and thickens slightly, 1½ to 2 hours on high or 3½ to 4 hours on low.

**2.** Serve warm with toothpicks for easy snacking. Leftover meatballs may be stored in an airtight container in the refrigerator for up to 4 days. Reheat on the stovetop in a saucepan over medium heat, stirring occasionally until the meatballs are warmed through, about 8 minutes.

### Remi's Recommendations

If you don't have a slow cooker, you can easily make these on the stovetop. In a large pot over medium heat, combine the jelly, barbecue sauce, and frozen meatballs and toss to coat. Cook, covered, stirring occasionally, until the meatballs are warmed through and the sauce becomes bubbly and thickens slightly, 25 to 30 minutes. If the sauce thickens before the meatballs are cooked, reduce the heat. Serve warm.

Growing up, I looked forward to this dish the most during the holidays. My mom had a little green recipe book she would pull out for Thanksgiving and Christmas that contained a recipe for a cheesy, crunchy potato casserole. Over the years, she would make "little Suz tweaks" that made it so much better—and now she's passed this recipe down to me. We're a family that welcomes all extra friends to our holidays, and most everyone who has come to a Cruz family holiday leaves begging for the recipe to make for their families—which I am now sharing with you. PSA: These are also called "funeral potatoes," I like to think, because of all the cheese, butter, sour cream, cheese, butter, cheese, more cheese, more butter. I guarantee any potato-lover will love them. Cal, my husband, can't believe how lucky I was to grow up eating this dish on the regular.

# SUZ'S CORNFLAKE POTATO CASSEROLE

### Serves 8

- 1 (16-ounce) container (about 2 cups) sour cream
- 2 cups (8 ounces) shredded cheddar cheese
- 1 (10.5-ounce) can condensed cream of chicken soup
- 1½ cups (3 sticks) plus 1 tablespoon unsalted butter, melted, divided
- 2 teaspoons garlic powder
- 2 teaspoons onion powder
- 1 teaspoon kosher salt, plus more as needed
- ½ medium yellow onion, finely chopped (about ½ cup)
- 3 garlic cloves, finely chopped
- 32 ounces frozen shredded hash browns
- 6 cups cornflake cereal

**1.** Preheat the oven to 350°F.

**2.** In a large bowl, combine the sour cream, cheese, soup, ½ cup of butter, the garlic powder, onion powder, and salt. Set aside.

**3.** In a medium skillet over medium heat, warm 1 tablespoon of butter, then add the onion and sauté until the onion just starts to brown, 4 to 5 minutes. Add the garlic and stir to combine. Cook until the garlic is fragrant, another 30 seconds, and remove from the heat.

**4.** Sprinkle the shredded hash browns evenly in a 9 x 13-inch casserole dish, breaking up any clumps that are stuck together with your hands.

**5.** Pour the sour cream mixture over the hash browns and spread evenly to coat. Do not stir this mixture with the potatoes (I know it seems crazy, but it will all melt down in the baking process!).

**6.** In a large bowl, combine the cornflakes with the remaining 1 cup of butter by pouring it evenly over the cereal, then sprinkle the cornflakes with a few pinches of salt and, using a rubber spatula, toss gently to coat. Top the potatoes with the buttered cornflakes, set the dish on a baking sheet, and cover the top with aluminum foil (this will allow the potatoes to cook through without burning the cornflakes!).

*(recipe continues)*

• • •

**7.** Bake until the cheese is bubbling and the potatoes are thoroughly warmed through, about 40 minutes, then remove the foil and bake until the cornflake topping gets crispy and turns dark golden on the edges, another 10 to 15 minutes.

**8.** Remove the dish from the oven and serve immediately. Leftovers may be stored in an airtight container in the refrigerator for up to 5 days. Reheat in the microwave or an oven preheated to 350°F until warmed through.

### Remi's Recommendations

You can easily make this dish ahead of time. Prep everything up until combining the cornflakes with butter. Refrigerate your potato/sour cream mixture in the baking dish for up to 3 days. When you are ready to bake it, toss the cornflakes with the butter, top the prepared potatoes, and bake as directed.

Smothered in more than a cup of melted garlic butter, these rolls make any holiday dinner that much more indulgent. I developed this recipe a few years ago and it has become an absolute favorite for any party I throw. While making rolls may sound intimidating, this recipe is almost foolproof because you don't have to make the rolls! The game changer: store-bought Hawaiian sweet rolls, you know, the ones you find in an orange King's Hawaiian-branded bag. This recipe is all about what you *do* with the rolls, which is dousing them in crazy amounts of garlic and butter. Served toasty and warm, these disappear so fast you may want to consider making a double (or triple) batch!

# BEST-EVER GARLIC BUTTER ROLLS

### Makes 24 rolls

- 1½ cups (3 sticks) unsalted butter, melted
- 10 large garlic cloves, minced or grated
- ¼ cup grated Parmesan cheese, plus more for garnish
- 3 tablespoons finely chopped fresh flat-leaf parsley, plus more for garnish
- 2 teaspoons garlic powder
- 1 teaspoon onion powder
- ½ teaspoon kosher salt
- Freshly ground black pepper
- 24 Hawaiian sweet rolls

**1.** Preheat the oven to 350°F. Line a baking sheet with parchment paper or foil.

**2.** In a medium bowl, stir together the butter, garlic, Parmesan, parsley, garlic powder, onion powder, salt, and a few pinches of pepper.

**3.** Place the rolls on the prepared baking sheet. Using a small, sharp knife, slice vertically into each roll to deepen the existing cut and spoon the butter mixture into the crevices. Brush the tops of the rolls generously with the butter mixture, too, reserving 2 to 3 tablespoons to brush on after baking.

**4.** Bake until the rolls look slightly toasted on the sides and when you press on the tops they no longer feel soft, about 10 minutes?

**5.** Once finished baking, brush the rolls with the reserved butter mixture, and sprinkle with Parmesan and parsley. The garlic rolls are best served immediately after baking.

#### LET'S HAM IT UP!
**Give your garlic butter rolls a hearty twist by adding ham and cheese.**
Using a serrated knife, cut each 12-roll loaf horizontally as if you were slicing a sub roll. Stir together ¾ cup Kewpie mayonnaise and 2 tablespoons sriracha and spread it on the insides of all four halves. Lay ½ pound sliced deli ham and ½ pound sliced Swiss cheese on the bottom halves of the rolls and put the second halves on top. Brush each loaf with the garlic mixture as directed above and bake for about 10 minutes, or until the cheese starts to melt. Brush the rolls with the remaining butter mixture, sprinkle with Parmesan, and serve immediately.

I didn't fully appreciate a crab rangoon until I met my husband. I had looked past them at every Chinese-American restaurant, but my view changed once I realized how simply perfect they are. They're creamy, crunchy, sweet, and savory all at the same time. I stick with imitation crab for the filling, which most restaurants use as well because it's cost effective. If you're feeling fancy, absolutely go ahead and sub in real lump or claw meat. Also, because I love things sweet, I add a dash of sugar to the filling. If you're strictly the savory type, leave it out. I like to serve rangoons with a sweet chili sauce to bring out the sweetness of the crab and cream cheese, but they also pair well with plum sauce or are great entirely on their own!

# FRIED CRAB RANGOONS WITH SWEET CHILI SAUCE

### Makes 24 rangoons

- 1 cup (8 ounces) cream cheese, softened
- 4 teaspoons soy sauce
- ½ teaspoon granulated sugar (optional)
- Kosher salt
- Freshly ground black pepper
- 4 ounces imitation crabmeat, minced (about ¾ cup)
- 2 medium green onions (white and green parts), chopped (about 2 heaping tablespoons)
- 1 medium garlic clove, minced or grated
- 24 wonton wrappers
- 2 quarts vegetable oil or other high-heat neutral oil, for frying
- ½ cup Thai sweet chili sauce, for serving

### Remi's Recommendations

For a healthier twist, air-fry the wontons at 350°F for 10 minutes, then turn them, spray them with oil, and air-fry until crispy and golden, another 10 minutes more.

**1.** In a medium bowl, stir together the cream cheese, soy sauce, sugar, if using, and a pinch or two each of salt and black pepper until well combined. Fold in the crab, green onions, and garlic until thoroughly combined.

**2.** Lightly flour a baking sheet or line with parchment paper.

**3.** Lay 1 wonton wrapper on a flat work surface and, using a pastry brush or your finger, lightly brush or dab all the edges of the wrapper with water. Put 1 tablespoon of the filling in the center of the wrapper. To make a star-shape, use your thumb and forefinger to pinch together each corner to meet in the center, pinching the seam between your fingers as you do so to seal in the filling. Sealing the wrappers tightly is key as you don't want the filling to leak out during frying. Place the sealed rangoon on the prepared baking sheet. Repeat the procedure using the rest of the wrappers and the filling.

**4.** In a large pot, using a candy thermometer, heat the oil to 350°F over high heat. (Your oil should be 2½ inches deep; if you don't have a candy thermometer, see page 23 for more on frying.) Working in small batches, using tongs or chopsticks, lower the rangoons into the oil and fry until golden brown, 2 to 3 minutes total. If you can, try to turn the wontons. They do bob and float because they're bottom heavy, so you can use the tongs or chopsticks to hold them down in the oil for 5 to 10 seconds to golden. Even if they aren't completely golden they will still be crispy.

**5.** Serve hot with the sweet chili sauce for dipping. Crab rangoons are best eaten soon after being fried.

LET'S GET HOSTING

Japan is one of my favorite places in the world. When I touch down in Tokyo, one of my first stops is always a convenience store or konbini (the Japanese term for convenience store) for all the deliciousness they have to grab and go. Whether it's a 7/11, Lawsons, or Family Mart, I saunter in for an egg salad sandwich and fried chicken because I can't resist the smell, especially the crispy, juicy karaage (Japanese fried chicken). While the original is deep-fried, I've come up with a healthier, air-fried version. And to me, it's not a compromise as it's crispy outside and juicy inside—and it transports me back to those lively, bustling streets of Japan.

# JAPANESE AIR-FRIED CHICKEN BITES

### Serves 4 to 6 as an appetizer/snack

- ⅓ cup soy sauce
- 2 tablespoons mirin
- 1 tablespoon plus 1 teaspoon granulated sugar
- 3 garlic cloves, minced or grated
- 4 boneless, skinless chicken thighs (about 1¼ pounds), cut into 2-inch pieces
- 1 cup potato starch
- 1 teaspoon garlic powder
- 1 teaspoon onion powder
- 1 teaspoon kosher salt
- Freshly ground white pepper
- High-heat cooking spray such as avocado oil
- ¼ cup Kewpie mayonnaise, for serving

1. In a medium bowl, combine the soy sauce, mirin, 1 tablespoon sugar, and the garlic. Stir to combine. Add the chicken pieces and toss to coat. Cover and set aside to marinate for 30 minutes.

2. In a second medium bowl, combine the potato starch, the reamaining 1 teaspoon sugar, the garlic powder, onion powder, salt and a few pinches of pepper and whisk to combine.

3. Preheat an air fryer to 375°F.

4. Using a fork, pierce a piece of chicken in the marinade, allowing the excess marinade to drip off, and dip it in the starch mixture, entirely coating all sides, and put it on a large plate or small sheet pan. Continue the process until all the chicken pieces are coated.

5. Spray all sides of the chicken pieces with oil, and transfer as many pieces of chicken that will fit into the air fryer basket.

6. Cook until the coating on the chicken is crispy and the pieces are cooked through, 8 to 10 minutes. When you cut into one, it should be white with no pink color and the juices should run clear. Repeat the cooking process until all the chicken is cooked.

7. Serve with a small dish of Kewpie mayo on the side. Leftover chicken may be stored in an airtight container in the refrigerator for up to 3 days. To reheat, warm the chicken in an air fryer preheated to 375°F until it's warmed through, about 4 minutes.

By now you probably get the idea that I love garlic and cheese. Actually, I'm OBSESSED. If I had to count, I bet over 60 percent of the recipes in this book have some form of garlic, or cheese, or both. Here I'm adding a third favorite thing to the mix: wings. (There's another wing recipe in this book, too, see page 147.) I like to say if a chicken wing wanted to be garlic bread, this is how it would taste. When buying wings, a party chicken wing pack means everything because they already come separated into drumettes and wingettes (also called flats), saving a lot of butchering time on your end. These make the best game-day snack and give Wingstop Garlic Parmesan wings a run for their money.

# GARLIC PARMESAN CHICKEN WINGS

## Makes about 12 wings

- 1 cup (2 sticks) unsalted butter
- 10 medium garlic cloves, minced
- ½ cup finely grated Parmesan cheese, plus more for garnish
- 1 tablespoon chopped fresh flat-leaf parsley, plus more for garnish
- ½ teaspoon kosher salt, plus more for seasoning
- Freshly ground black pepper
- 2 quarts vegetable oil or other high-heat neutral oil, for frying
- 2 pounds (about 12 pieces) bone-in chicken drumettes and wingettes
- ½ cup all-purpose flour

**1.** In a large microwave-safe bowl (you are going to toss the wings in this bowl later), melt the butter for about 1 minute on high, then stir in the garlic, Parmesan, parsley, salt, and a few pinches of pepper and set aside.

**2.** In a large pot or Dutch oven, over high heat, using a candy thermometer, bring the oil to 350°F (your oil should be 2½ inches deep, see page 23 for more on frying). Line a plate with paper towels and set aside.

**3.** Using paper towels, pat the wings dry. In a medium bowl, generously sprinkle the wings with salt and pepper and toss to coat. After you've seasoned the wings, sprinkle them with the flour and toss to coat.

**4.** When your oil is to temperature, fry the wings in batches until golden and crispy, about 15 minutes. Using tongs, transfer the wings to the prepared plate.

**5.** When you are done frying all the wings, add them to the bowl with your sauce and toss to coat. (If the sauce is no longer liquid, heat it up in the microwave on high for 30 seconds before adding the wings.)

**6.** To serve, transfer the wings to a platter and pour the extra sauce over them. Sprinkle with Parmesan and parsley before serving. Leftover wings may be stored in an airtight container in the refrigerator for up

*(recipe continues)*

• • •

to 4 days. To reheat, spread the wings on a baking sheet and warm in a 350°F oven, flipping them halfway through, until re-crisped and warmed through, 10 to 15 minutes. You may also reheat them in an air fryer preheated to 375°F until re-crisped and warmed through, 5 to 7 minutes.

### Remi's Recommendations

Not ready to fry? You may also oven bake your wings, then toss them in the garlic butter sauce.

To do so, preheat the oven to 450°F and, depending on the size of your baking sheets, fit with a wire rack(s) and follow steps 1 and 3 above (obviously skip warming the oil). Instead of frying, bake the wings until crispy and golden, about 40 minutes total, flipping them after 20 minutes of baking. When cooked, toss them in the garlic butter and serve as directed.

As a California girl, fresh strawberries remind me of warm summers, the beach, and yummy desserts. I have always been a huge strawberry fan—I remember my mom pulling over at the local strawberry field to pick up cartons of the freshest, juiciest, reddest berries. Now you'll find me growing my own luscious strawberries, peaches, and tomatoes in my garden every summer. This dessert is a wonderful way to turn ripe strawberries into something even more tasty. If you can't get fresh berries, frozen ones work equally well for these bars. The jammy, berry center sandwiched between a rich, buttery vanilla-y base and crumbly streusel topping tastes like the equivalent of a big, sweet hug.

# SWEETEST STRAWBERRY BUTTER CAKE BARS

### Makes 24 bars

- 1½ cups (3 sticks) unsalted butter, softened, divided, plus more for greasing the pan
- 2 cups granulated sugar, divided
- 2 large eggs
- 1 teaspoon pure vanilla extract
- 2¾ cups all-purpose flour, divided
- 1 teaspoon kosher salt, plus more as needed
- 2 teaspoons baking powder, divided
- 32 ounces (about 3 cups) frozen or fresh hulled strawberries, chopped
- Grated zest and juice from ½ an orange (1½ teaspoons zest and about ¼ cup juice)
- Vanilla ice cream, for serving (optional)

**1.** Preheat the oven to 350°F. Grease a 9 x 13-inch baking pan with butter and set aside.

**2.** In the bowl of a stand mixer with a paddle attachment, cream together 1 cup of butter and 1 cup of sugar until light and fluffy.

**3.** Add the eggs one at a time, beating well after each addition. Stir in the vanilla.

**4.** Gradually add 1½ cups of flour, the salt, and 1 teaspoon of baking powder. Using a rubber spatula, scrape down the sides of the bowl as needed. Mix well until a thick dough forms.

**5.** Press the dough evenly into the prepared baking pan, using an offset spatula to smooth it out. Bake the crust until it just starts to turn golden, about 25 minutes. Remove it from the oven and set aside to cool.

**6.** In a saucepan over low heat, combine the strawberries, orange zest, orange juice, ½ cup of sugar, and a pinch of salt.

**7.** Using a wooden spoon or potato masher, gently mash and stir the strawberries as they start to soften (if using fresh strawberries, add ⅓ cup water to help create a sauce).

*(recipe continues)*

LET'S GET HOSTING

● ● ●

**8.** Once the berries become saucy, increase the heat to medium-high and bring the mixture to a boil. Continue to boil for 1 to 2 minutes, stirring constantly, then reduce the heat to low. Continue to simmer until the strawberries are fully softened and the sauce has thickened and reduced to about 4 cups, about 10 minutes. Remove from the heat and allow to cool.

**9.** Meanwhile, in a medium bowl, combine the remaining ½ cup butter, ½ cup sugar, 1¼ cups flour, a pinch of salt, and the remaining 1 teaspoon baking powder. Stir together, then, using your hands, clump the mixture together until it's crumbly.

**10.** Pour the cooled strawberry sauce evenly over the cooled crust, then sprinkle the crumble mixture over the top.

**11.** Bake until the top is golden brown, another 45 to 50 minutes.

**12.** Allow the pan to cool, then slice into 24 bars. Enjoy warm with a scoop of vanilla ice cream, if desired, or serve at room temperature. Store the bars in an airtight container in the refrigerator for up to 3 days.

I love a THICK, cakey cookie! During my first trip to New York with my best friend, Alisha, she kept raving about the best chocolate chip cookie from a bakery called Levain. She demanded I try it, and, boy, was she right—it was the best cookie I ever had. At the time, Levain was only available in NYC, so I developed this recipe to have a little piece of Levain at home in LA. This recipe uses cold butter straight from the fridge, so you can make these BIG, gooey chocolate chip cookies at any time, without softening butter in advance. But in order to get the cakey-ness that I'm talking about, you do need to chill the dough for at least eight hours.

# WORLD'S BEST CAKEY CHOCOLATE CHIP COOKIES

### Makes 8 cookies

- 1 cup (2 sticks) cold unsalted butter, cut into small cubes
- 1 cup packed light brown sugar
- ½ cup granulated sugar
- 2 large eggs
- 2 tablespoons corn syrup
- 1 tablespoon pure vanilla extract
- 1¼ cups cake flour
- 1½ cups all-purpose flour
- 1 teaspoon baking powder
- 1 teaspoon baking soda
- 1 teaspoon kosher salt
- ½ cup milk chocolate chips or chunks
- ½ cup dark chocolate chunks

**1.** In the large bowl of a stand mixer fitted with a paddle attachment, cream the butter, brown sugar, and granulated sugar on medium speed, scraping down the sides as needed, for about 3 minutes, or until light and fluffy.

**2.** Add the eggs, one at time, mixing after each addition until fully incorporated. Add the corn syrup and vanilla and mix again until well combined.

**3.** Next, add the cake flour, all-purpose flour, baking powder, baking soda, and salt and run the mixer on low until the dry ingredients are just incorporated, using a rubber spatula to scrape down the sides as needed.

**4.** Using a rubber spatula, fold in the chocolate chips and chocolate chunks (you can also add these in and run the mixer on low until they are *just* mixed in).

**5.** Using a ½-cup measure, scoop out 5 ounces of the dough (no worries if you don't have a scale, it's about an even ½ cup) and roll to form 2-inch-tall cylindrical-shaped mounds. Place them in a covered container or resealable bag in the refrigerator for 8 hours or overnight. This helps the flavors to deepen and results in a thicker cookie. You may bake them right away, but you'll get a thinner cookie that is still delicious but not cakey.

*(recipe continues)*

●●●

**6.** When ready to bake the cookies, preheat the oven to 400°F. Line 2 baking sheets with parchment paper and place the dough rounds on the baking sheets, leaving 3 inches of space between each cookie (I typically fit 4 cookies per sheet because they spread).

**7.** Bake until golden brown, about 12 minutes.

**8.** Cool before serving. The cookies are best served the day they are baked. Leftovers may be stored in an airtight container for up to 3 days.

Picture this: school is back in session, you've got a backpack full of fresh notebooks and new gel pens, you've watched all of Alisha Marie's back-to-school hacks, and you're ready to start the new school year, but what are you packing for snack time? Whenever my mom packed me a Little Debbie Cosmic Brownie, I knew I was about to be the coolest kid at the lunch table. And while you can't go wrong with the classic store-bought version, this homemade twist on a childhood favorite is worth the effort. I use Dutch-process cocoa here, richer in color and flavor than most natural mass-market cocoa powders, to balance the bar's sweetness—and cater to a more grown-up palate (though kids will love them, too). I find these just as dense and fudgy as I remember the original (or even better, to be honest!), topped with the requisite rich ganache and signature rainbow chips.

# OUT-OF-THIS WORLD GALAXY BROWNIES

*Makes 24 brownies*

### FOR THE BROWNIES
Baking spray
1 cup (2 sticks) unsalted butter, melted
3 large eggs plus 1 egg yolk
1½ cups granulated sugar
¾ cup packed light brown sugar
1 teaspoon pure vanilla extract
1 cup all-purpose flour
¾ cup Dutch-processed cocoa powder
1 tablespoon cornstarch
½ teaspoon kosher salt
⅓ cup vegetable oil

### FOR THE FROSTING
¾ cup semi-sweet chocolate chips
½ cup heavy cream
1 tablespoon corn syrup
¼ cup rainbow-colored candy-coated chocolate chips (see page 106)

**1.** Preheat the oven to 350°F. Line a 9 x 13-inch pan with parchment paper overhanging on two sides, then coat the pan and the parchment with baking spray.

**2.** Make the brownies: In a large mixing bowl, whisk together the butter, eggs, and egg yolk, then add the granulated sugar, brown sugar, and vanilla and whisk until smooth. Next whisk in the flour, cocoa powder, cornstarch, and salt until fully combined and smooth. Lastly, stir in the oil until fully incorporated.

**3.** Using a rubber spatula, spread the batter evenly into the prepared pan and bake until a toothpick inserted into the center of the brownies comes out clean, 30 to 35 minutes. Once baked, set the pan of brownies in the refrigerator to cool for at least 30 minutes before topping with the ganache frosting.

**4.** Make the frosting: In a double boiler set over medium heat, combine the semi-sweet chocolate chips, heavy cream, and corn syrup. Whisk often until the chocolate chips melt and the frosting is smooth and thick, 5 to 8 minutes. Pour the frosting over the cooled brownies and, using an offset spatula, smooth to create an even layer. Sprinkle with the rainbow-colored candy-coated chocolate chips.

*(recipe continues)*

• • •

**5.** Chill the brownies in the refrigerator briefly before cutting into 24 squares. Store in an airtight container in the refrigerator for up to 5 days.

### Remi's Recommendations
### Rainbows, Smiles, and Sprinkles

If you know Little Debbie Cosmic Brownies, you know the candy-coated pieces sprinkled across the sweet snack are key to the signature look. You can find the rainbow-colored candy-coated chocolate bits in bulk on Amazon or at craft stores (they are similar to candy-coated mini chocolate chips but are more irregularly shaped). You can also use mini M&Ms for a similar effect. Or use whatever sprinkles you have on hand.

If I had to choose my favorite type of cookie, it'll always be a sugar cookie. Plain, rolled in sprinkles, I'll take any sugar cookie any day. The nutty richness of brown butter takes these soft, chewy sugar cookies to the next level. If you're in a hurry, melted butter works as well as brown butter, you just won't get the nuanced nutty flavor. I like rolling the dough balls in nonpareils or sparkly colored sugar for holidays and special occasions.

# BROWN BUTTER SUGAR COOKIES

### Makes 16 cookies

- 1 cup (2 sticks) unsalted butter
- 2 cups all-purpose flour
- 1 teaspoon baking powder
- 1 teaspoon baking soda
- ½ teaspoon kosher salt
- 1½ cups granulated sugar
- 2 large eggs plus 1 yolk
- 2 teaspoons pure vanilla extract
- ½ to 1 cup nonpareils, sparkling sugar, or sprinkles, for rolling (you may also use granulated sugar here as well)

**1.** In a small saucepan over low heat, melt the butter (it's best not to use a dark-coated pan as it's harder to see when the butter turns brown). Shake the pan and cook until the butter begins to brown and develops a nutty aroma, 8 to 10 minutes.

**2.** Once browned, remove the butter from the heat and let cool completely.

**3.** In a medium bowl, whisk together the flour, baking powder, baking soda, and salt. Set aside.

**4.** In a large bowl, whisk together the sugar, eggs, egg yolk, vanilla, and cooled brown butter (be sure to scrape in all the brown bits) until light and fluffy.

**5.** Gradually add the dry ingredients, stirring until a dough forms.

**6.** Using a tablespoon measure, scoop out a heaping spoonful (you actually want balls that are 2 tablespoons, which is about equivalent to a heaping tablespoon; if you have a 2-tablespoon scoop, you can use that, too). Using your hand, form the dough into balls and put them on a baking sheet if you have room in your fridge for it, otherwise put the balls on a plate. Wrap the sheet tray or plate in plastic wrap and chill for at least 30 minutes or up to two days.

**7.** When you are ready to bake the cookies, preheat the oven to 350°F and line two baking sheets with parchment paper, which may include the baking sheet from the fridge.

*(recipe continues)*

• • •

**8.** Pour your coating of choice into a small bowl. Completely roll each chilled dough ball in the coating and place them on the prepared cookie sheet about 2 inches apart. Using the palm of your hand, slightly press down on the dough balls for a flatter cookie.

**9.** Bake until the edges turn slightly golden (in my opinion it's better to underbake these for a softer cookie, overbaking will make them crispy), about 12 minutes.

**10.** Remove from the oven and let the cookies cool on the baking sheet for a few minutes before transferring them to a wire rack to completely cool. Store the cookies in an airtight container for up to 3 days at room temperature.

### Remi's Recommendations

If you crave late-night cookies, this recipe could be your answer. The dough balls freeze great. After chilling them (and before rolling them in your coating of choice), transfer the dough balls to a resealable bag or airtight container. When ready to bake, pull the dough balls straight from the freezer, roll in your coating of choice, and bake according to the directions, adding a few minutes of baking time.

If you haven't heard, Twix is my absolute favorite candy bar. During the Covid-19 pandemic, I started exploring ways to get all the flavors of a Twix bar while giving them a healthier twist... and along came dates. I genuinely believe dates are underrated. They're like nature's candy. They are naturally sweet and have a caramel-like texture, which is the star of this recipe. I also gave the well-known American candy my spin by adding almond extract and orange zest to the cookie crust. You can leave it out for a more traditional Twix taste. Whatever you do, though, don't leave out the flaky salt—it's a must. Cal isn't super into healthy alternatives, but whenever I tell him I'm making these, he can't help but get excited!

# Ooey Gooey Chocolate Caramel Candy Bars

*Makes 24 bars*

**FOR THE CARAMEL**
15 large pitted dates
¼ cup hot water, plus more for soaking

**FOR THE COOKIE BASE**
¾ cup finely ground almond flour
¾ cup all-purpose flour
3 tablespoons granulated sugar
Kosher salt
1½ teaspoons grated orange zest
¼ cup refined coconut oil, melted
1 teaspoon almond extract
1 teaspoon pure vanilla extract (optional)

**FOR THE TOPPING**
1 cup (6 ounces) semi-sweet chocolate chips
2 teaspoons refined coconut oil
Flaky salt

1. Preheat the oven to 350°F. Line an 8-inch-square pan with parchment paper overhanging on two sides. (If you want thicker bars, you can use a loaf pan.)

2. Place the dates in a heatproof bowl and cover them with boiling water. Soak for 10 minutes.

3. Make the cookie base: In a medium bowl, whisk together the almond flour, all-purpose flour, sugar, 2 generous pinches of salt, and the orange zest.

4. Stir in the coconut oil, almond extract, and, if using, the vanilla extract until thoroughly incorporated. The mixture will be very crumbly. You can test that the ingredients are fully combined by pressing a fingerful of the mixture between your fingers. It should stick together.

5. Transfer the crumbly cookie base to your prepared pan and press it down firmly and evenly (the back of a spatula works great for this), trying to eliminate any holes. Bake until the edges start to turn golden, 18 to 20 minutes. Allow the base to cool for 10 minutes.

6. Meanwhile, make the "caramel": Drain the dates and put them in a high-speed blender or food processor with the hot water. If using a blender, run it on low to chop up the dates, then increase the speed to high. Process until you have a smooth paste.

*(recipe continues)*

LET'S GET HOSTING

• • •

**7.** Spread the date caramel mixture over the cooled cookie layer and put the pan in the freezer for 10 minutes.

**8.** While the bars chill, make the topping: In a heatproof bowl, combine the chocolate chips and coconut oil and microwave on high for 1 minute. Stir until smooth. If the chocolate is not completely melted, heat at additional 30-second intervals until the chocolate becomes smooth.

**9.** Pour the melted chocolate over the chilled date caramel layer. Sprinkle with flaky salt. Freeze until the chocolate is set, about 30 minutes.

**10.** Using the two "handles" of the parchment, gently lift the bars out of the pan and transfer them to a cutting board. Using a large knife, cut the bars in half, and then each half in half again, and each quarter in half one more time to get 8 long bars. I then cut each of those long bars into 3 "Twix-size" bars to get 24 bars total. Store in a sealed container in the refrigerator for up to 4 days.

# *Happy to Be Here!*

# WEEKEND DRUNCHIE BRUNCHES

My superhero power is going out and having the best night, then coming home and making delicious drunchies for my friends. If you don't know what drunchies are, it's all the food you crave when you are drunk (and truthfully, what I want to eat when I'm sober, too). In this chapter I've rounded up those recipes, the ones I make when I'm drunk, the ones I make to feed my hangover the day after or my girlfriends for brunch—and then we get drunk on mimosas. The recipes in this chapter are fun, even if they may take a little more time to make (especially if you've got a headache). Drink responsibly. Cook responsibly.

Crispy Cheddar Hash Brown Avocado Toast   118

Crunchy Cereal French Toast with Homemade Whipped Cream   121

Matcha Latte Pancakes   125

Crab Cake Eggs Benedict with Homemade Hollandaise   127

BBB (Best Breakfast Burger)   131

Fruity-Flavored Cereal Milk-Glazed Pancakes   133

Homemade Biscuits and Sage Sausage Gravy   137

Croissant Breakfast Bake   139

If you have any guests who love avocado toast, they will be uberimpressed by this elevated spin on an LA classic. The hash brown base is definitely more labor intensive than popping bread in a toaster, but it's worth every minute of effort. The hash browns are fantastic on their own as well, or serve them up with some crispy bacon, pancakes, or any other of your brunch faves. If you want to turn your brunch into a drunchies moment, whip up a batch of mimosas or spike some green juice.

# CRISPY CHEDDAR HASH BROWN AVOCADO TOAST

### *Makes 6 avocado toasts*

- 3 russet potatoes (about 2 pounds), peeled, shredded, and put in a bowl of cold water
- 7 large eggs, divided
- 2 tablespoons all-purpose flour
- 1 cup shredded white cheddar cheese
- 2 garlic cloves, minced or ½ teaspoon garlic powder
- 2 teaspoons chopped fresh rosemary
- 1½ teaspoons kosher salt, plus more for seasoning
- 1 teaspoon onion powder
- ¼ teaspoon freshly ground black pepper, plus more for seasoning
- ¼ cup avocado oil or other high-heat oil, for frying, plus more as needed, divided
- 2 small avocados
- 1 to 2 tablespoons chili crisp, for serving

**1.** Drain the shredded potatoes and rinse them again with cold water (keeping them in water helps prevent them from browning). Using a clean kitchen towel, squeeze them dry.

**2.** Crack 1 egg into a large mixing bowl and lightly whisk. Add the dried shredded potatoes and stir to combine. Sprinkle the flour over the potatoes and stir again to coat. Add the cheese, garlic, rosemary, salt, onion powder, and pepper and stir until thoroughly combined.

**3.** Next, using about a ½ cup of the mixture per hash brown, use your hands to form 4-inch patties. You should get 6 patties. (You can form them into thinner patties for a crispier hash brown.) It's okay to squeeze out the additional liquid when forming the patties. Gently place the formed patties on a baking sheet.

**4.** In a medium skillet, over medium-high heat, pour 3 tablespoons of avocado oil and heat until it starts to shimmer. Using a spatula, gently slide as many hash browns as you can fit comfortably into the pan and cook until they are brown and crispy on the bottom, about 8 minutes. Then flip the hash browns and fry until they become crispy on the other side, about another 8 minutes or so. Remove the hash browns from the pan and transfer them to a paper towel–lined plate to absorb the excess oil. Repeat until all the "potato toasts" are cooked.

**5.** Prep your toast toppers by slicing the avocados and dividing the slices among the 6 toasts.

*(recipe continues)*

•••

**6.** Next, cook the remaining 6 eggs. In the same skillet (if there are any potato bits in the skillet, wipe those out first) over medium heat, add the remaining oil, and heat until it starts to shimmer. Crack as many eggs into the pan as will fit and season with salt and pepper. For perfectly runny eggs (which are a must in my opinion), cook uncovered for 3 minutes, then cover and cook until the whites are just set, an additional 1 to 2 minutes. Using a spatula, gently slide 1 cooked egg on 1 toast and repeat until all the eggs are cooked and all the toasts are topped.

**7.** To serve, drizzle with the chili crisp and salt and pepper to taste, and enjoy. The hash browns can be cooked up to 1 day in advance and stored in the refrigerator until ready to serve. (They can also be frozen.) To reheat, place the hash browns on a parchment-lined baking sheet and heat in a 350°F oven until warmed through, 8 to 10 minutes. Make the eggs as directed above.

### Remi's Recommendations
For extra crispy hash browns, cook your "toasts" in a greased air-fryer basket at 375°F for 15 minutes. Flip the patties and cook until crisp and golden, an additional 3 to 5 minutes. Use as directed above.

I LOVE cereal. Period. I'll take cereal anything: milk & cereal-flavored ice cream, cornflake cookies, even cereal-milk lattes. I am NOT, however, a fan of ordinary french toast. When I first moved to LA, I went to brunch with my girlfriends and was mind-blown to see Cereal French Toast on the menu. I immediately ordered it, and I thoroughly enjoyed my french toast experience for the first time ever. This recipe is such a fun twist on your average french toast, and whether you love or hate the original stuff, you will love this. The sweet cornflakes take usually plain french toast to the next level, adding extra crunch, sweetness, and deliciousness.

# CRUNCHY CEREAL FRENCH TOAST WITH HOMEMADE WHIPPED CREAM

### Serves 4

- 3½ cups heavy cream
- 6¼ cups Frosted Flakes cereal (about ¾ of a 12-ounce box) or other sweetened cereal of choice, divided
- 6 large eggs
- 1 tablespoon granulated sugar
- 1 teaspoon pure vanilla extract
- Kosher salt
- 4 tablespoons (½ stick) unsalted butter, plus more as needed
- 8 pieces (¾- to 1-inch thick) brioche bread
- 1 pint fresh berries such as blueberries or raspberries, for topping

**1.** Preheat the oven to 300°F. If you have a rack that fits in a baking sheet, get that ready to keep your french toast warm, or you can just use a baking sheet, too. The rack helps keep the coating crispy.

**2.** In a medium bowl, combine the heavy cream and 3¼ cups of cereal, making sure the cereal is fully submerged. Refrigerate for 15 minutes.

**3.** Meanwhile, to a resealable plastic bag, add the remaining 3 cups of cereal, seal, and whack it using something heavy, like a rolling pin or even your fist, until the cereal is crushed with visible pieces remaining (you don't want to pulverize the cereal to dust). Pour the crushed cereal onto a rimmed dinner plate.

**4.** In a medium shallow bowl large enough to dip the bread into, crack the eggs and whisk until thoroughly combined and frothy. Add the sugar, vanilla, and 2 pinches of salt and whisk again.

**5.** After the cereal is done soaking, pour through a fine-mesh strainer into a liquid measuring cup or pitcher, pushing the cereal with the back of the spoon to press out all the liquid. You should get about 2¼ cups of cream. Dispose of the cereal solids or eat the soft, cream-soaked deliciousness.

*(recipe continues)*

● ● ●

**6.** Add 1¼ cups of the strained cream to the egg mixture and whisk to combine. Into the bowl of a stand mixer fitted with a whisk attachment or a medium mixing bowl, pour the remaining 1 cup of cream, and beat until soft peaks appear. Put the whipped cream in the fridge to chill.

**7.** In a large skillet over medium-low heat, melt 2 teaspoons of butter or more as needed to coat the bottom of the pan.

**8.** Dip a piece of bread into the egg mixture, soaking each side until the center is fully saturated, about 15 seconds (it will almost feel like the bread is going to fall apart; you may want to use a spatula to transfer it, or use both hands to support it in the center), then dip the bread into the crushed cereal to coat both sides. Transfer the bread to the skillet. Repeat the process with a second piece of bread if it'll fit comfortably in the pan. Cook until golden on the bottom, 4 to 5 minutes, then flip and cook until the second side is golden. Don't be tempted to turn up the heat. You are going for low and slow here, so the eggy center cooks. The oven will also finish off baking the center. Transfer the cooked french toast to the baking sheet and put it in the oven to warm while you repeat the process, adding more butter to the pan and dipping and cooking the rest of the bread.

**9.** To serve, transfer the cooked and warmed french toast to a platter, and either top with fresh berries and the cereal-sweetened whipped cream or serve them on the side. French toast is best eaten the day it is made.

I'm not a big pancake person, so when I do make them, I like to make them a little more interesting than your average pancake. Inspired by my love for anything matcha, these green pancakes, topped with a dreamy dollop of mascarpone cream, have a naturally earthy flavor that will instantly wow your taste buds (and/or your guests'). I'm particular about my matcha green tea powder. There are different grades including ceremonial, premium (also called daily or traditional), and culinary, with the first being the highest grade, and the most complex, which is why I give a range of matcha amounts in the recipe. You may need to adjust the amount based on the grade you use. Go slowly when adding the matcha, and add more to your taste. No matter how you flip 'em or the matcha you choose, these pancakes are next level.

# MATCHA LATTE PANCAKES

### Makes 6 large pancakes

**FOR THE MATCHA LATTE CREAM**

- ½ cup heavy cream
- ½ cup mascarpone
- 2 tablespoons powdered sugar
- ½ teaspoon matcha green tea powder

**FOR THE PANCAKES**

- 1 cup cake flour
- 1 cup all-purpose flour
- ½ cup granulated sugar
- 1 teaspoon to 1 tablespoon matcha green tea powder, depending on the grade (see headnote), plus more for serving
- ½ teaspoon baking soda
- ½ teaspoon baking powder
- ½ teaspoon kosher salt
- 1½ cups whole milk
- 2 large eggs
- 1 teaspoon pure vanilla extract
- 6 tablespoons unsalted butter, melted, divided

**1.** Make the matcha latte cream: In the bowl of a stand mixer fitted with a whisk attachment or medium bowl with a hand mixer, combine the heavy cream, mascarpone, powdered sugar, and matcha powder. Whisk until smooth and thickened and the cream holds stiff peaks. Refrigerate until ready to use.

**2.** Preheat the oven to 250°F.

**3.** Make the pancakes: In a large bowl, whisk together the cake flour, all-purpose flour, sugar, matcha powder, baking soda, baking powder, and salt. In a separate bowl, whisk together the milk, eggs, and vanilla until combined. Pour the liquid ingredients into the center of the dry ingredients and whisk until just incorporated. Pour in 3 tablespoons of butter and whisk again until smooth.

**4.** In a large skillet, preferably nonstick, over medium heat, pour in 1 tablespoon of butter and swirl to evenly coat the bottom of the pan. When the pan is hot (a drop of water will sizzle on the pan when it's hot), pour ½ cup of batter into the pan, forming a 5- to 6-inch circle. Reduce the heat and cook until bubbles form, 3 minutes. Flip and cook the pancake on the other side until it's golden brown and cooked through, another 3 minutes or so. Reduce the heat if your pancakes are getting too brown outside and not cooking through in the center. You'll likely need to reduce the heat by the second pancake. Transfer the cooked pancake to a baking sheet and keep warm in the oven.

*(recipe continues)*

WEEKEND DRUNCHIE BRUNCHES

**5.** Repeat the process, adding a teaspoon or more of butter as needed with every pancake, and cook the remaining batter.

**6.** To serve, put the warm pancakes on a serving platter and top with dollops of the matcha cream, which will slowly melt over the pancakes. If you'd like, garnish by sifting a little matcha over the top of the cream. The pancakes are best eaten when they are made.

### Remi's Recommendations
#### Subbing Cake Flour

I use cake flour in this recipe because it has a low protein content (which means less gluten) that yields a tender result. If you don't have cake flour, though, you can use all-purpose flour with no other changes in the recipe and still get a good pancake *or* if you have cornstarch and all-purpose flour, you can *make* cake flour.

To make cake flour, add 1 cup all-purpose flour to a medium bowl. Remove 2 tablespoons of the flour and add 2 tablespoons cornstarch. Sift the flour/cornstarch mixture 2 to 3 times before using. Spoon the cake flour substitute into a measuring cup, level, and use as directed.

Seriously decadent, this spin on a traditional eggs benedict was inspired by a version from one of my favorite restaurants, Cinnamon's, the sweet mom-and-pop restaurant on O'ahu, Hawaii. With crispy crab cakes and a velvety hollandaise, this is a combination I often crave on hungover mornings. While I think it's best served on a fresh homemade biscuit base (try my recipe on page 137); a toasted English muffin or bagel work if you're short on time. And speaking of time, this is a slow morning kind of recipe as there are several steps, including poaching eggs. I promise it's easier than it sounds, and once you have the technique down, you'll want poached eggs on everything. These crab cakes are amazing, I'm talking WOW, and worth the effort.

# CRAB CAKE EGGS BENEDICT WITH HOMEMADE HOLLANDAISE

*Makes 6 crab cake benedicts*

**FOR THE CRAB CAKES**

2 large eggs

2 tablespoons mayonnaise

1 teaspoon Dijon mustard

1½ teaspoons Old Bay seasoning

⅛ teaspoon kosher salt, plus more as needed

Freshly ground black pepper

3 green onions (white parts only), finely chopped (about 1 heaping tablespoon)

1 small shallot, minced (about 1 tablespoon; optional)

1 pound lump crab meat

⅓ cup panko breadcrumbs

2 tablespoons chopped fresh flat-leaf parsley

3 tablespoons avocado or vegetable oil, for frying, plus more as needed

**1.** Make the crab cakes: In a large bowl, whisk together the eggs, mayonnaise, mustard, Old Bay seasoning, salt, and 2 pinches of black pepper until smooth and well combined. Taste and adjust for seasoning as needed with salt and pepper. Stir in the green onions and, if using, the shallot.

**2.** Add the crab meat, panko, and parsley and gently fold it into the egg/mayo mixture, taking care not to break up the crab meat too much.

**3.** With clean hands, form 6 same-size patties and place them on a baking sheet or plate that will fit in your refrigerator and chill for at least 30 minutes.

**4.** Make the hollandaise sauce: In a high-power blender, combine the egg yolks, lemon juice, mustard, and a pinch or two of cayenne pepper and run on high until combined, about 10 seconds. Now, with the blender running on medium, slowly (and I mean slowly), add the butter drop by drop through the top of the blender. Once the sauce starts to thicken, you can add the rest of the butter in a thin stream (as opposed to droplets). Keep blending until all the butter is added and the sauce is creamy. Add a pinch or two of salt to taste. Set aside.

*(recipe and ingredients continue)*

**FOR THE HOLLANDAISE SAUCE**

4 large egg yolks

4 teaspoons lemon juice, plus more as needed

2 teaspoons Dijon mustard

Cayenne pepper

½ cup (1 stick) unsalted butter, melted

Kosher salt

**FOR ASSEMBLY**

3 biscuits (see page 137) or toasted English muffins, sliced in half

1 large tomato, thinly sliced

Kosher salt

Freshly ground black pepper

3 tablespoons white vinegar

6 large eggs

1 to 2 tablespoons chopped fresh chives, for garnish

• • •

**5.** Preheat the oven to 250°F. Set a large pot of water on the stove over high heat for poaching the eggs.

**6.** Fry the crab cakes: In a large skillet, heat the oil, or enough to generously coat the bottom of the pan, over high heat until it shimmers. Using a spatula, gently slide the crab cakes into the skillet (as many as will fit), and fry until the bottoms start to turn golden brown, about 4 minutes, then, using a spatula, very gently turn the crab cakes and fry on the other side for another 4 minutes or so, or until also golden brown. Transfer the cooked crab cakes back to the baking sheet and keep warm in the oven while you poach the eggs.

**7.** Set out 6 plates and place half of a biscuit face-up on each plate. Top each with a tomato slice and season with a pinch of salt and pepper.

**8.** Poach the eggs: Your large pot of water should be boiling by now, or if not, when it does, reduce the heat so the water remains at a gentle simmer. Add the vinegar to the water.

**9.** Crack one egg into a small bowl or ramekin. Stir the water a few times to create a whirlpool effect. Gently tip the egg into the center of the whirling water and very gently simmer until the whites are set and the yolk is still runny, about 3 minutes. Right before your egg is done cooking, remove a crab cake from the oven and place it on top of the tomato. Using a slotted spoon, carefully remove the egg from the water and place it on top of the tomato. You can cook more than one egg at time, but getting a few whirlpools going at once can be challenging. Either way, repeat the process until all the eggs are cooked and placed on top of the tomato.

**10.** Season the eggs with a pinch or two of salt and pepper followed by a drizzle of hollandaise sauce. Garnish with the fresh chives and serve. Assembled Crab Cake Eggs Benedict are best eaten right away.

### Remi's Recommendations

For easy hosting, the crab cakes, the hollandaise—and even the eggs—can be made up to 1 to 2 days ahead. For the crab cakes, fry and then cool and refrigerate them in an airtight container until ready to use. Same with the hollandaise and the eggs. To store the eggs, transfer them to a container with cool water (they'll be floating in the container).

To reheat the crab cakes: Warm in a 350°F oven until crisped up and warmed through, 8 to 10 minutes. You could also warm the crab cakes in an air fryer at the same temperature for about 5 minutes.

To reheat the hollandaise: Warm the sauce in a double-boiler over very low heat and whisk until it just becomes warm. Do not heat the hollandaise quickly or over high heat as this can cause the sauce to separate or get lumpy. If this happens, add a few drops of cold water and whisk again. The sauce can seem temperamental so really go slow with the reheating.

To reheat the poached eggs: Fill a bowl with very hot water and, using a slotted spoon, lower the eggs into the water until heated through, about 30 to 60 seconds.

My all-time drunk meal of choice is the Denny's Slam Burger. I lived in Downtown LA for five years, and after every night out with my best friends, Alisha and Oli, you could almost always find us at the Denny's that was about 200 feet from my apartment. Nothing hits the spot at 2 a.m. quite like a juicy, greasy burger loaded with crispy hash browns and melted cheese, then topped with a perfectly fried egg. It's a late-night dinner/early morning breakfast on a bun. To set the scenario for success, I call for frozen premade patties and frozen hash browns. I don't want any drunchie mishaps. And you'll see I'm loose with the seasoning measurements because TBH, is anyone pulling out measuring spoons when they're tipsy? While these burgers are pretty foolproof, if you are a bit inebriated, maybe enlist a slightly more sober friend to help you out!

# BBB (BEST BREAKFAST BURGER)

### Makes 2 burgers

- 1½ cups (about 5 ounces) frozen shredded hash browns
- Lawry's Seasoned Salt
- 2 to 3 tablespoons extra-virgin olive oil, divided
- 2 frozen beef patties
- 2 slices white American cheese
- 2 slices yellow American cheese
- 2 large eggs
- Kosher salt
- Freshly ground black pepper
- 1 tablespoon unsalted butter
- 2 soft burger or brioche buns, sliced in half
- Ketchup and mayonnaise, for serving
- 4 slices cooked pork bacon (optional)

**1.** In a large skillet over medium heat, add the hash browns, season with a few pinches of Lawry's Seasoned Salt, and cook, stirring occasionally, for about 3 minutes, or until the hash browns have defrosted and become soft. Add 1 tablespoon of olive oil and toss to coat. Spread out the hash browns in a single layer and allow them to cook, undisturbed, until they start to crisp up on the bottom, about 4 minutes. Using a spatula, turn the hash browns and cook until they crisp up on the other side, another 4 minutes or so. Transfer the cooked hash browns to a large plate and set aside.

**2.** Sprinkle the burger patties on each side with a few pinches of Lawry's Seasoned Salt. Wipe out the skillet, set it over medium-high heat, add 1 to 2 teaspoons of olive oil to the pan, and heat until it shimmers. When the pan is nice and hot, add the patties and cook until they are browned on the bottom, 5 to 7 minutes, then flip them, place 1 piece each of white and yellow cheese on top of each patty, cover the skillet with a lid, and cook to your desired doneness, another 5 to 7 minutes for medium rare, depending on the thickness of your patties. Transfer the burgers to the plate with the hash browns.

*(recipe continues)*

**3.** In the same pan, over medium-high heat, add another 2 teaspoons of oil and crack your eggs directly into the pan. Sprinkle each egg with a pinch or two of salt and pepper. For a sunny-side-up egg, cook until the whites are set and the yolks remain slightly runny, 2 to 3 minutes. If you prefer an over-easy egg, flip the eggs when the whites are about halfway cooked. Transfer the cooked eggs to a plate while you toast the buns.

**4.** You are almost there! I hope you're still with me. In the same skillet, melt the butter. Place the buns in the pan, cut-side down, and cook until they just start to become golden, a minute or two.

**5.** Now you are ready to assemble your burger: Spread some ketchup and mayo on each bun, then add your patty, a stack of hash browns, bacon, if using, and top with a fried egg. Dig in immediately!

### Remi's Recommendations

If you don't have Lawry's Seasoned Salt, feel free to use a few pinches garlic powder, onion powder, salt, and pepper instead. Combine and taste, then add a pinch more of whatever is needed until you are happy with the flavor. You got this!

You may find it odd for someone who claims *not* to love pancakes (as I noted in Matcha Latte Pancakes, page 125, headnote) to include two pancake recipes in this book. The reason is that these pancakes are so much more than just plain pancakes! Also, I know pretty much everyone else loves pancakes and everyone in my life went crazy for this recipe, so I knew I had to include it. My matcha ones are an edible version of a latte, and these, well, these are a fun version of a fun cereal! Feel free to sub in any of your favorite cereals as these are incredibly customizable. If you're wondering why I add vinegar to these pancakes, it's a buttermilk hack (read: you don't need to buy buttermilk). Instead, the vinegar chemically reacts with the milk and does the same thing as buttermilk, which tenderizes pancakes, making them lighter and fluffier. Of course, if you do have buttermilk on hand, feel free to swap it in for the whole milk.

# FRUITY-FLAVORED CEREAL MILK-GLAZED PANCAKES

### *Makes 6 pancakes*

**FOR THE PANCAKES**

1 cup whole milk

1 tablespoon white vinegar

2 cups all-purpose flour

⅓ cup granulated sugar

½ teaspoon baking powder

½ teaspoon baking soda

½ teaspoon kosher salt

2 large eggs

1 teaspoon pure vanilla extract

6 tablespoons unsalted butter, melted, divided

1¾ cups Fruity Pebbles or other sugar-sweetened cereal, coarsely crushed, divided

**FOR THE GLAZE**

1 cup powdered sugar

2 tablespoons whole milk

½ teaspoon pure vanilla extract

**1.** Preheat the oven to 250°F.

**2.** Make the pancakes: In a small bowl, stir together the milk and vinegar and set aside for about 8 minutes, or until it thickens slightly.

**3.** In a large bowl, whisk together the flour, sugar, baking powder, baking soda, and salt. In a separate bowl, whisk together the thickened milk/vinegar mixture, the eggs, and vanilla until combined. Pour the liquid ingredients into the center of the dry ingredients and whisk until just incorporated. Pour in 3 tablespoons of butter and whisk again until smooth.

**4.** Using a rubber spatula, fold in 1½ cups of Fruity Pebbles.

**5.** Make the glaze: In a small bowl, whisk together the powdered sugar, milk, and vanilla until smooth. Set aside.

**6.** In a large skillet, preferably nonstick, over medium heat, pour in 1 tablespoon of butter and swirl to evenly coat the bottom of the pan. When the pan is ready (a drop of water will sizzle on the pan when it's hot), pour ½ cup of the batter into the pan, forming a 5- to 6-inch circle.

*(recipe continues)*

• • •

Reduce the heat and cook until bubbles form, 2 to 3 minutes. Flip and cook the pancake on the other side until it's golden brown and cooked through, another 3 minutes or so. Reduce the heat if your pancakes are getting too brown outside and not cooking through inside. You'll likely need to reduce the heat by the second pancake. Transfer the cooked pancake to a baking sheet and keep warm in the oven.

**7.** Repeat the process, adding 1 teaspoon of butter to the pan for each pancake, and cook the remaining batter.

**8.** When ready to serve, arrange the pancakes on a platter and drizzle with the glaze and sprinkle with the remaining ¼ cup of crushed cereal. These pancakes are best eaten within minutes of cooking.

If you know me, you know I love comfort food, and a good biscuit is definitely a classic Southern comfort food. I like getting my hands into making biscuits—creating butter shards by squeezing cold cubes into the flour mixture contributes to this biscuit's flaky texture. I find biscuits are a great base for so many things: honey, butter and jam, and savory things like my Crab Cake Eggs Benedict (page 127), and here, a rich, thick gravy. This is a good dish for serving a large group. They are worth every bit of effort. Let's get baking those biscuits!

# HOMEMADE BISCUITS AND SAGE SAUSAGE GRAVY

*Makes 8 biscuits with gravy*

**FOR THE BISCUITS**

- 2 cups all-purpose flour, plus more for dusting
- 1 teaspoon baking powder
- 1 teaspoon baking soda
- 1 teaspoon kosher salt
- 1 cup (2 sticks) cold unsalted butter, cut into ½-inch cubes
- 1 large egg, lightly whisked
- ½ cup buttermilk
- Flaky salt

**FOR THE GRAVY**

- 8 ounces ground pork sausage or Italian sausage
- 2 tablespoons all-purpose flour
- 1 cup whole milk, plus more as needed
- 1 cup heavy cream
- ½ teaspoon ground sage
- ¼ teaspoon kosher salt
- Freshly ground black pepper
- 1 to 2 tablespoons chopped fresh flat-leaf parsley, for garnish (optional)

**1.** Preheat the oven to 350°F. Line a baking sheet with parchment paper and set aside.

**2.** Make the biscuits: In a large bowl, whisk together the flour, baking powder, baking soda, and salt.

**3.** Add half of the butter cubes and toss to coat. Using your two thumbs and forefingers, squeeze the cubes into the flour mixture to create shards the size of a pea. Add the remaining butter cubes and again, using your fingers, make some shards that are slightly larger, like the size of a dime.

**4.** Sprinkle the egg and buttermilk over the flour/butter mixture, and, using a fork, toss until the mixture is completely moistened.

**5.** Using your hands, very gently bring the dough together into a ball, working to preserve as many butter shards as possible. Turn out the dough onto a lightly floured workspace. Using your hands, very gently press the dough into a 7 x 4-inch rectangle that is about 1 inch high. Cut the dough into 8 squares and, using your hands, turn the squares clockwise to form a round-ish biscuit. Transfer the biscuits to the prepared baking sheet. Sprinkle with flaky salt. Bake until the biscuit tops turn golden, 20 to 23 minutes.

*(recipe continues)*

• • •

**6.** Make the gravy: In a large skillet over medium heat, add the sausage and cook, stirring often, and breaking up the sausage into small pieces. Once the sausage is no longer pink and the fat has rendered, let the sausage sit undisturbed to brown on one side, 2 to 3 minutes. Then turn the sausage so it browns on the other side and you have sausage crumbles, another 3 to 4 minutes.

**7.** Reduce the heat to low and sprinkle the flour evenly over the crispy sausage. Stir, scraping up the brown bits for extra flavor, about 1 minute.

**8.** Pour in the milk and heavy cream, increase the heat to medium, and stir until the mixture comes to a slow simmer. Reduce the heat to low, add the sage, salt, and a few pinches of pepper and stir to combine. Continue to cook over low, stirring continuously, until your gravy is the desired consistency. If it's too thick, add more milk as needed. The gravy does thicken as it cools.

**9.** Serve the gravy in a bowl, or split the warm biscuits and spoon the gravy over them and sprinkle with the fresh parsley, if desired. The biscuits are best eaten the day they are made.

In our house, this bake is a Christmas morning crowd-pleaser. I often prep it the night before, and on Christmas morning, I pop it into the oven as we sip coffee and sit around, sharing stories and laughter. The combination of buttery croissants, eggs, cheese, and sausage gives it a breakfast sandwich feel that is especially satisfying and comforting—and croissant-centric. The flaky cut-up crescents are *just* held together by the eggs, meaning you get some nice, crispy pieces that aren't soaked with egg. This dish has become such a wonderful tradition in our home. I can't wait to continue it with kids one day.

# CROISSANT BREAKFAST BAKE

## Serves 6 to 8

- 1 tablespoon unsalted butter, plus more for greasing the pan
- 6 croissants, roughly chopped
- 12 large eggs
- ¼ cup heavy cream
- 1 teaspoon garlic powder
- 1 teaspoon Italian seasoning (optional)
- 1 teaspoon kosher salt, plus more for seasoning
- ¼ teaspoon freshly ground black pepper, plus more for seasoning
- 1 medium yellow onion, diced (about 1 cup)
- 1 pound ground pork or turkey sausage
- 2 cups (8 ounces) shredded cheddar or Swiss cheese

### Remi's Recommendations

You may assemble this breakfast bake ahead. To do so, prepare the sausage/onion mixture and whisk up the egg mixture and store them both in separate containers in the refrigerator. You may prep the croissants in the buttered dish and cover with foil (it's okay for the croissants to dry out some, they'll crisp up nicely in the oven). When you are ready to bake the dish, follow the instructions above.

1. Preheat the oven to 350°F.

2. Generously butter a 9 x 13-inch pan or casserole dish and spread the croissant pieces in a thin layer.

3. In a large bowl, combine the eggs, heavy cream, garlic powder, Italian seasoning, if using, the salt, and pepper and whisk until everything is well combined and almost frothy. Set aside.

4. In a medium skillet over medium heat, melt the butter and add the onion. Cook until the onion just starts to soften, about 3 minutes. Crumble in the sausage and, using a spoon, break it apart into small pieces. Continue cooking and stirring until the sausage is browned and no pink remains, about 8 minutes. Season with a pinch or two each of salt and pepper. Using a slotted spoon, spread the sausage/onion mixture over the croissants.

5. Next, pour the egg mixture evenly over the sausage/onion mixture. There will be just enough egg mixture to barely cover the pan and that's okay. Use the back of a spoon or offset spatula to push the ingredients down so that they are submerged and the croissants are soaking up the liquid. Sprinkle the cheese evenly over the entire pan.

6. Bake until the eggs are set and the cheese just starts to turn golden, about 30 minutes.

7. Serve warm. Leftovers may be stored in the refrigerator for up to 3 days. Reheat in a 350°F oven until warmed through, about 10 minutes. An air fryer works great for reheating, too.

# MY FAVORITE KOREAN DISHES

If you watch my vlogs, you know I say, "This is my favorite" about pretty much everything. *However,* the recipes in this chapter really *are* my all-time favorites. Just like I couldn't ever choose a favorite between my three dogs, Luna, Momo, and Daisy, I couldn't choose just one best-loved among these dishes—they are all special and each one means so much to me. You'll find classics from my childhood—like Galbi (page 169), Mom's Kimchi-Jjigae (page 176), and Tteokbokki (page 145)—that make me feel warm, cozy, and comforted inside; and there are fun takes on Korean street food inspired by my trips to Seoul, like Crunchy Street Dogs (page 155) and Korean Street-Style Ham and Cheese Sandwiches (page 185). I've also included some of my beloved fusion dishes, my creative takes on more authentic-style Korean recipes. One of my favorite parts about Korean cuisine is the mix of salty and sweet, sweet and spicy, spicy and salty. More often than not, a Korean dish combines more than one element of flavor.

For those of you new to Korean cooking, there's a quick ingredients primer in the front of the book (see page 19). For me, cooking big portions of Korean food is in my genes so many of these recipes yield large portions. If you are only cooking for a few people, consider halving a recipe or freezing any extra as meal prep if it's too big for your purposes.

Tteokbokki (Spicy Stir-Fried Rice Cakes)   145

Soy Garlic Hot Honey Chicken Wings   147

Korean Soy-Marinated Eggs   150

Budae-Jjigae (Korean Army Stew) Crispy Potstickers   153

Crunchy Street Dogs   155

Korean Buffalo Cauliflower Bites   159

Rosé Udon with Crispy Pork Belly   161

Kimchi Fried Rice with an Egg   165

Cheesy Kimchi Pork Belly Panini   166

Galbi (Marinated Short Ribs)   169

Galbi-Jjim (Braised Beef Short Rib Stew)   171

Mom's Kimchi-Jjigae (Kimchi Stew)   176

Sweet and Spicy Gochujang Meatballs   179

Korean Fried Chicken Sandwich with Asian Pear Slaw   181

Korean Street-Style Ham and Cheese Sandwiches with Sweet Sriracha Mayo   185

Korean Cheesy Corn Casserole   186

I'm a texture person so I find tteokbokki (pronounced duk-bo-key), with fresh, chewy rice cakes, also called tteok, extremely satisfying to eat—some say it reminds them of a thick rice pasta. You can find the key ingredient for this dish, the tteok, made from steamed rice, at most Asian markets, either fresh or refrigerated, and you will likely find them in many shapes. Traditionally, tteokbokki is made using the plain, small, cylinder-shaped rice cakes (tteok do not resemble crispy, popped American rice cakes in any way). While every recipe in this chapter feels like my favorite, this one really is my ALL-TIME favorite. It's one of those dishes that evokes many memories for me. As a kid, I got extremely excited when the Crock-Pot of tteokbokki arrived at a family hangout. I would pluck out the fish cake (see Remi's Recommendations, page 146) and eggs. The sweet and spicy sauce and satisfying chew give this a real comfort-food feel—it's something I always order when I'm sick or craving Korean food. Don't let the name fool you, though. This dish has just the right amount of spice: not too much, but enough to give it a little kick. (There are some places in Los Angeles where their extra mild is too spicy for me!) P.S.: Try adding a little mozzarella cheese on top—it's my secret to making this dish even more decadent, and don't forget the fish cake and eggs!

# TTEOKBOKKI (SPICY STIR-FRIED RICE CAKES)

*Serves 6 to 8*

**FOR THE RICE CAKES**

3 cups warm water

1 pound fresh or frozen cylinder tteok (rice cakes)

**FOR THE SAUCE**

3 tablespoons soy sauce

3 tablespoons toasted sesame oil

2 tablespoons gochujang paste

2 tablespoons granulated sugar

Gochugaru coarse chile flakes, plus more as needed (optional)

**FOR THE MEAT**

2 tablespoons toasted sesame oil, divided

1 (8-ounce) boneless ribeye steak, cut into bite-size cubes

**1.** Fill a large bowl with the warm water and soak the rice cakes until softened, 10 to 15 minutes or as directed on the package, then drain.

**2.** Make the sauce: In a medium bowl, whisk together the soy sauce, sesame oil, gochujang, sugar, and a pinch of gochugaru, if desired. Taste for your desired spiciness and add a pinch or more of gochugaru, if using, to taste. Set aside.

**3.** Cook the meat: In a large shallow pot or high-sided skillet, heat 1 tablespoon of sesame oil over medium high-heat, until it starts to shimmer. Add the cubed ribeye, sprinkle with a few pinches of salt and pepper, and cook until the meat has browned on all sides and is medium-rare inside, 3 to 4 minutes if your pan is nice and hot, which it should be! Tongs or a large fork are great for turning the meat. Transfer the meat

*(recipe and ingredients continue)*

MY FAVORITE KOREAN DISHES  **145**

Kosher salt

Freshly ground black pepper

½ medium yellow onion, thinly sliced

½ small cabbage, outer leaves removed, cored, and cut into 1 x 2-inch strips (about a heaping 2 cups)

6 garlic cloves, minced or grated

3 cups water

2 hard-boiled eggs (page 23)

1 cooked fish cake, chopped

3 green onions (white and green parts), cut on the bias

1 tablespoon sesame seeds

### Remi's Recommendations

Korean fish cakes can be found in most Asian markets. There are many different kinds, and they vary in texture, from chewy to rubbery. Some are pink and white, some are swirled, and others are plain brown. It's really up to you what texture you prefer so I recommend trying a few different ones until you find what you like through trial and error. I will usually grab a variety and throw them into my dishes to add different textures, and the pink and white ones are so cute to snap pics of!

• • •

to a large bowl and set aside. (You'll be adding the cooked onion and cabbage to this bowl in a bit.)

**4.** In the same shallow pot or skillet over medium-high heat, add the remaining 1 tablespoon of sesame oil and the onion, using tongs to stir-fry until the onion just starts to soften, 2 to 3 minutes, then add the cabbage and continue to cook until the cabbage just starts to soften but does not become translucent, about 3 minutes. If the pan feels dry, add a few tablespoons of water, or more as needed, to keep the onion and cabbage from charring (the water helps loosen any char from the pan as well). Lastly, reduce the heat to medium, add the garlic, and cook until it's fragrant, about 30 seconds. Transfer the cooked onion/cabbage mixture to the same bowl with the cooked ribeye.

**5.** In the same large shallow pot or high-sided skillet that you cooked the meat and vegetables in, pour in the water (no need to wash out the pan) and heat over medium-high. Add the sauce you made earlier to the water, whisk to combine, and bring the mixture to a boil. Add the soaked and drained rice cakes and bring the water back to a boil, then reduce the heat to medium low and simmer until the sauce has thickened and the rice cakes absorb some liquid to get nice and plump, about 20 minutes. The sauce should feel more creamy than watery.

**6.** Add the meat/onion/cabbage mixture to the saucy rice cakes along with any juices that have accumulated and stir to combine. Lastly, add the eggs (I put them in whole, like my aunt always does, but feel free to cut them in half or slices if you'd like) and fish cake and stir again to coat. Heat until everything is warmed through, 3 to 4 minutes.

**7.** To serve, divide the tteokbokki among four bowls and top with the green onions and a sprinkle of the sesame seeds and enjoy. Tteokbokki can be stored in an airtight container for up to 3 days. Reheat in the microwave or on the stovetop in a skillet until heated through.

Drunk, sober, or in between, I'm always down for some chicken wings, and this recipe highlights my favorite way to prepare them—with an Asian flare! Korean fried chicken is such a unique and special type of fried chicken, and some of my most fond memories from Korea are eating it with my mom, dad, and Alisha. This recipe was featured in my first-ever episode of *Cooking with Remi*, and the wings have become a staple in the Cruz-Parsons household. The heat from the hot honey paired with the savory soy-garlic flavor is the perfect combo of sweet *and* spicy. You can fry the wings in oil, or they also crisp up nicely in an air fryer or oven as well. However you make them, they're truly some of the best wings you'll ever have.

# SOY GARLIC HOT HONEY CHICKEN WINGS

### *Makes about 12 wings*

**FOR THE SAUCE**

- 2 tablespoons water
- 1 tablespoon cornstarch
- 2 tablespoons unsalted butter
- 10 garlic cloves, finely chopped (about 4 tablespoons)
- 1 tablespoon fresh ginger, peeled and finely chopped or grated (about a 2-inch piece)
- ½ cup soy sauce
- 3 tablespoons Hot Honey (page 24) or store-bought
- 3 tablespoons granulated sugar
- 2 tablespoons toasted sesame oil
- 2 tablespoons chili oil

**FOR THE WINGS**

- 2 quarts vegetable oil or other high-heat neutral oil, for frying
- ½ cup cornstarch
- 1 teaspoon paprika
- ¾ teaspoon garlic powder
- ¾ teaspoon onion powder
- Kosher salt

**1.** Make the sauce: In a small bowl, whisk together the water and cornstarch until smooth to form a slurry. Set aside.

**2.** In a small pot over medium-low heat, melt the butter, then add the garlic and ginger and cook until fragrant, about 3 minutes. Add the soy sauce, honey, sugar, sesame oil, and chili oil, and cook, stirring intermittently, until the mixture starts to simmer, about 5 minutes. Pour the slurry into the sauce, reduce the heat to low, and continue to whisk while it simmers and thickens slightly, another 1 to 2 minutes. Pour the sauce into a large mixing bowl. (You are going to toss the wings in this bowl with the sauce.) Set aside.

**3.** Make the wings: In a medium pot over medium-high heat, pour in the vegetable oil and heat to 350°F (see page 23 for more on frying).

**4.** While the oil heats, prep the wings. In a medium shallow bowl, whisk together the cornstarch, paprika, garlic powder, onion powder, a few generous pinches of salt, and a few pinches of pepper. Using your hands, thoroughly coat the dry wings in the cornstarch/spice mixture and place them in a single layer on a baking sheet.

*(recipe and ingredients continue)*

MY FAVORITE KOREAN DISHES

Freshly ground black pepper

2 pounds (about 12 pieces) bone-in chicken drumettes and wingettes, patted dry with a paper towel

Furikake, for garnish

1 to 2 teaspoons sesame seeds, for garnish (optional)

Minced dried garlic, for garnish (optional)

• • •

**5.** When the oil is heated, working in small batches, use tongs to lower the wings into the oil and fry until golden and crispy, 7 to 8 minutes per side.

**6.** Using tongs or a spider, transfer the fully cooked wings to the bowl with the sauce, and toss to coat the wings evenly in the sauce.

**7.** To serve, transfer the saucy wings to a platter and sprinkle with furikake and/or, if using, sesame seeds and dried garlic. The wings are best eaten right away.

As a true egg lover, I find this recipe takes one of life's simplest pleasures and converts it into something even better. Inspired by the delicious banchan (side dishes) I had as a kid, this umami-packed egg is a go-to for me whenever I'm craving something with bold, savory flavors. The eggs soak up the soy sauce, garlic, and sesame oil, transforming them into a rich snack or topping. Although you can buy ready-made eggs like these in Asian markets, I prefer homemade ones because they're so easy to make and are an inexpensive way to elevate some dishes. I learned the hard way that these eggs have a shelf life of about 2 to 3 days in the fridge (although they often don't even make it that long with Cal and me scarfing them down). If you let the eggs sit in the fridge for too long, they tend to taste weird and get rubbery.

# KOREAN SOY-MARINATED EGGS

### Makes 8 eggs

- 8 large eggs
- 1 cup soy sauce
- ½ cup granulated sugar
- ½ cup water
- ¼ cup mirin
- 8 medium garlic cloves, minced
- 1 tablespoon toasted sesame oil
- 3 green onions (white and green parts), chopped into 1-inch pieces
- 1 to 2 tablespoons black sesame seeds, for garnish (optional)

**1.** Fill a large pot with water and bring it to a boil over medium-high heat. Gently lower the eggs into the boiling water, reduce the heat, and gently simmer for 8 minutes. While the eggs boil, prepare an ice bath (a large bowl with water and ice). Using a slotted spoon, transfer the eggs from the boiling water to the ice bath and allow them to fully cool. Peel the cooled eggs and dispose of or compost the shells. Set aside.

**2.** In a large lidded gallon container or jar, whisk together the soy sauce, sugar, water, mirin, garlic, and sesame oil until the sugar dissolves. Add the green onions and eggs. Refrigerate and allow the eggs to marinate for 2 days, shaking a few times each day to make sure the eggs marinate evenly, for the best flavor.

**3.** To serve, garnish with a sprinkle of the sesame seeds, if desired. The eggs are best eaten within 3 days.

LET'S GET COOKING

I like to call this my double-fusion dish. Budae-jjigae is a well-known stew (*budae* translates to army or military unit and *jjigae* means stew), like Mom's Kimchi-Jigae (page 176), that originated in South Korea after the Korean War when food was scarce. Koreans used processed meats, like Spam and sausages available from the American bases, in their traditional stews and a fusion was born. I've taken this combination one step further and folded all those ingredients into a dumpling filling that's hearty and flavorful, and takes fusion fare to the next level. When I make these dumplings (also called mandu), I like to make *a bunch* and freeze them for later (see Let's Freeze Potstickers, page 154). To make these potstickers extra indulgent, deep-fry them for an extra crunch (see page 23).

# BUDAE-JJIGAE (KOREAN ARMY STEW) CRISPY POTSTICKERS

### Makes 30 potstickers

**FOR THE DIPPING SAUCE**

3 tablespoons soy sauce

3 tablespoons mirin

1 tablespoon granulated sugar

**FOR THE POTSTICKERS**

1 (4-ounce) pork belly chunk, cut into very small cubes

3½ ounces Spam, cut into very small cubes

1 cup cabbage, finely diced (about a ¼ of a small cabbage)

½ cup kimchi, finely diced

¼ small white onion, finely diced (about 2 tablespoons)

1 tablespoon soy sauce

1 to 2 teaspoons gochugaru coarse chile flakes

1 teaspoon granulated sugar

2 ounces dried ramen noodles (about half a standard noodle block), crushed

**1.** Make the sauce: In a small bowl, stir together the soy sauce, mirin, and sugar and set aside.

**2.** Make the potstickers: In a large nonstick skillet over medium heat, add the pork belly and Spam and cook until the fat starts to warm and sizzle, about 3 minutes. Then add the cabbage, kimchi, and onion and cook, stirring occasionally, until the veggies are softened and the meat is crispy, 8 to 10 minutes.

**3.** Add the soy sauce, 1 to 2 teaspoons of gochugaru depending on how spicy you'd like the mixture to be, and the sugar and stir to coat. Next add the crushed ramen and corn and stir until everything is well combined. Remove the filling from the heat and allow it to cool to the touch.

**4.** To fill the gyoza, place 1 wrapper on your work surface, dip your finger in a small bowl of water, and, with your finger, dampen the entire edge of the wrapper. Add 1 heaping teaspoon of filling to the center of the wrapper and seal the edges. You can pleat your potsticker by folding it in half, and pinching it in the center where the two sides meet. Next,

*(recipe and ingredients continue)*

MY FAVORITE KOREAN DISHES

¼ cup canned corn, drained

30 gyoza rounds (about 5 ounces, half a standard pack)

2 tablespoons vegetable oil

½ cup water

1 green onion (green part only), cut on the bias, for garnish

• • •

using your thumb and your forefinger, make 2 to 3 pleats on each side of the original center pinch. Repeat with the rest of the wrappers and filling until all the wrappers are used.

**5.** Wipe out the same large nonstick skillet that you used to cook the filling and set it over medium-high heat, pour in the oil, and heat until the oil shimmers. Add half the potstickers to the pan in a circular pattern, creating 2 rings of potstickers.

**6.** Cook until the bottoms turn golden brown, about 2 minutes. Add the water to the pan (stand back as the pan will sputter when the water hits the oil), and immediately cover with a lid. Steam until the liquid evaporates, about 5 minutes. Remove the cover and check to make sure the gyoza skins are completely translucent. Any sign of white means that the skins are not cooked through. Pull out one potsticker and cut in half to make sure the filling is cooked through.

**7.** Continue the cooking process, adding more water as needed, until all the potstickers are cooked.

**8.** Serve immediately with the dipping sauce and garnish with the green onion. Leftover dumplings may be refrigerated for up to 4 days. To reheat, put the dumplings in a microwave-safe dish, sprinkle with water, and cover with a damp paper towel. Heat on high at 20-second intervals until the dumplings are heated through.

### Remi's Recommendations
#### Pork Belly Hack!
To make chopping pork belly easier, throw it in the freezer for 20 minutes for an easier chop!

## LET'S FREEZE POTSTICKERS

Line a baking sheet or plate that will fit in your freezer with parchment paper. Place the uncooked potstickers in a single layer (not touching each other) on the baking sheet and freeze until solid. Once frozen, transfer the potstickers to a resealable plastic bag or lidded container. When you are ready to cook the frozen potstickers, there's no need to defrost them. Simply cook the potstickers as directed in the recipe but add a few more minutes of cooking time.

It's no secret that I absolutely LOVE Korean street food. Whenever I touch down in Seoul, the Myeongdong night market is a must-stop for me. I enjoy all the shops and bright lights, and especially the food carts, which serve up the most mouthwatering fare that often features the newest in innovative trends. The Korean street dog blew up in America a few years ago, and if you've ever tried one, you understand why. You can choose cheese or a hot dog as your base, and then that is rolled in a unique batter that is soft and bready inside yet gives the most delicious crunch. Though, what sets Korean corn dogs apart from American corn dogs is their toppings (and Korean dogs usually use rice or wheat flour in their batter, not cornmeal!). You can roll Korean street dogs in crushed ramen, potatoes, or my favorite—sugar. It's so simple but the results are such a wonderful salty and sweet combination that it has to be tried to be understood!

# CRUNCHY STREET DOGS

*Makes 8 to 10 crunchy skewers*

- 1¼ cups warm water
- 2 tablespoons granulated sugar, plus ½ cup for coating
- 1 (¼-ounce) packet dry yeast
- 2 cups all-purpose flour
- 2 teaspoons kosher salt, divided
- 8 (8- to 10-inch) bamboo skewers
- 4 hot dogs, cut into 1½- to 2-inch pieces
- 4 string cheese sticks, cut into 1½- to 2-inch pieces
- 2½ to 3 quarts vegetable oil or other high-heat neutral oil, for frying
- 1 cup panko breadcrumbs
- Ketchup and mustard, for serving (optional)

1. In a large mixing bowl, whisk together the water and the 2 tablespoons sugar and sprinkle with the yeast. Whisk again until the yeast and sugar are dissolved. Let the mixture sit until bubbles form, about 8 to 10 minutes.

2. Once the yeast bubbles, add the flour and 1 teaspoon of salt. Using a rubber spatula, stir until well combined and the dough comes together in a ball with no dry bits remaining. Cover the dough with a kitchen towel, set the bowl in a warm place, and let it rise for 30 to 40 minutes.

3. While you are waiting for the dough to rise, skewer the hot dogs and cheese by piercing one piece of hot dog vertically with the point of a skewer and threading it onto the skewer, followed by one piece of cheese also threaded vertically. Repeat to skewer all the hot dog and cheese pieces, mixing and matching as you like. You can thread all dog, all cheese, or some of both on one skewer. Refrigerate the skewers until you are ready to dip and fry them.

4. Meanwhile, in a medium pot, heat the oil to 350°F over medium-high heat (see page 23 for more on frying).

*(recipe continues)*

● ● ●

**5.** Once the dough has risen, pour the panko into a shallow dish and pour the ½ cup sugar in a second shallow dish. Set the dish with the sugar aside.

**6.** Next, dip a skewer into the risen dough, twirling it until fully coated. The dough will be thick, so if needed, use your hands to help mold the dough around the meat and/or cheese.

**7.** Roll the dough-coated skewer in the panko until fully covered. Make sure any dough around the cheese is well sealed to avoid leaks.

**8.** Using tongs, lower a completed skewer into the heated oil and fry until golden brown, about 3 minutes.

**9.** To serve, roll the hot golden dog or cheese in the sugar for added sweetness, then top with mustard and ketchup, if desired. Deep-fried hot dogs and cheese are best eaten right away.

Living in LA, I experienced a wave of cauliflower everything—cauli rice, cauliflower pizza crust, and of course Buffalo cauliflower bites. It was on menus, at markets, and everywhere in between. I'm a huge fan of Erewhon's Buffalo cauliflower, which is just the right amount of crispy, crunchy, and spicy. As I do, I took that inspo and made my own. This time, with a Korean twist. Honestly, I think I might like this more than Buffalo chicken wings, and you know I LOVE my wings (page 95 and 147). Also, if you don't have the ingredients for the sauce, consider dousing or dipping the fried cauli with any premade sauce you have on hand like barbecue sauce, wing sauce, or even a drizzle of Hot Honey (page 24).

# KOREAN BUFFALO CAULIFLOWER BITES

*Serves 4 as a snack or appetizer*

### FOR THE SAUCE

- 3 tablespoons unsalted butter
- 2 green onions (white and green parts separated), white parts chopped, for the sauce; the green parts sliced on the bias, for garnish
- 2 medium garlic cloves, minced
- ¼ cup gochujang paste
- ¼ cup honey
- 2 tablespoons soy sauce
- 2 tablespoons mirin
- Kosher salt
- Freshly ground black pepper

### FOR THE CAULIFLOWER

- 1½ to 2 quarts vegetable oil or other high-heat neutral oil, for frying
- 1 cup all-purpose flour
- 1 cup potato starch
- 1 teaspoon garlic powder
- 1 teaspoon onion powder
- 1 teaspoon kosher salt

**1.** Make the sauce: In a small saucepan over low heat, melt the butter. Add the white parts of the green onions and cook until just softened, about 3 minutes. Add the garlic, and stir and cook until it becomes fragrant, another minute or so.

**2.** Whisk in the gochujang, honey, soy sauce, mirin, and a few pinches of salt and pepper, and continue to whisk until smooth. Increase the heat if needed to bring the sauce to a slow simmer, then remove the sauce from the heat and set aside.

**3.** Make the cauliflower: Heat the oil in a medium pot over medium-high heat to 350°F (see page 23 for more on frying). Fit a baking sheet with a cooling rack and set aside.

**4.** In a large mixing bowl, whisk together the flour, potato starch, garlic powder, onion powder, salt, and pepper.

**5.** Slowly pour the club soda into the flour mixture and whisk until smooth. The batter should be slightly thick, like buttermilk. Add a few ice cubes to keep the batter cold.

*(recipe and ingredients continue)*

MY FAVORITE KOREAN DISHES

½ teaspoon freshly ground black pepper

1½ cups club soda or seltzer water

A few ice cubes

½ head cauliflower, cored and cut into bite-size pieces

1 to 2 tablespoons sesame seeds, for garnish

• • •

**6.** Using tongs, a fork, or chopsticks, dunk each cauliflower piece into the batter, completely coating it, and carefully lower it into the oil. Repeat the process until you have a small batch of cauliflower frying in the pot, about 5 or 6 pieces total. Avoid overcrowding. The pieces shouldn't be touching. Cook until parts of the coating start to turn golden brown, 5 to 7 minutes. Note that the coating pretty much stays white and will only brown in certain parts. Using tongs or a spider, transfer the fried cauliflower pieces to the prepared baking sheet, and continue the dipping and frying process until all the cauliflower is fried.

**7.** In batches, add the fried cauliflower pieces to the sauce and, using tongs or chopsticks, lightly toss the cauliflower to coat it with the sauce.

**8.** To serve, transfer the sauced cauliflower to a bowl or platter and garnish with the reserved sliced green onions and the sesame seeds. The cauliflower is best eaten right away.

This creamy, spicy udon dish is an elevated version of the viral Tiktok Buldak Spicy Carbonara Ramen I love so much. Of course, you could go to the store and buy Samyang's Buldak prepared Carbonara Hot Sauce. Still, this homemade version is super easy to make, and you can adjust the spice level to suit your taste (Buldak is known for their extremely spicy products!). This rosé sauce gets its kick from two signature Korean seasonings: gochujang and gochugaru (see page 19). The heavy cream balances out the smoky-sweet spice and melds with the garlic and onions to create a rich, decadent sauce with just enough heat, perfect for coating the udon noodles. I top it all off with crispy pork belly and a soft-boiled egg for the perfect blend of textures and flavors, all in one bite!

# ROSÉ UDON WITH CRISPY PORK BELLY

### Serves 4

- 2 (9-ounce) bricks frozen udon noodles
- 8 ounces skinless, boneless pork belly, cut into ½-inch pieces
- 1 to 2 tablespoons vegetable oil
- 1 small white onion, thinly sliced into ½ moons (about 1 heaping cup)
- 2 tablespoons minced garlic (about 6 to 7 large cloves)
- 1 green onion (white and green parts separated), both finely chopped
- 1 tablespoon gochujang paste
- 2 to 3 teaspoons gochugaru coarse chile flakes
- 1½ teaspoons toasted sesame oil
- 1 teaspoon granulated sugar
- 1 teaspoon soy sauce
- ½ cup heavy cream
- Kosher salt
- Freshly ground black pepper
- 2 soft-boiled eggs (page 23), cut in half
- Black sesame seeds, for garnish

**1.** Fill a large bowl with cold water and add the frozen noodles, allowing them to thaw, for about 10 minutes.

**2.** Fill a large pot with water and set it over high heat, cover, and bring it to a boil for cooking the noodles.

**3.** In a large sauté pan over medium-low heat, cook the pork belly until it's crispy and golden brown, 6 to 8 minutes. Transfer the cooked pork belly to a paper towel–lined plate and leave any pork fat in the pan. Add the vegetable oil as needed to equal about 2 tablespoons of fat total, then increase the heat to medium.

**4.** Add the onion and cook until it just starts to soften, 3 to 4 minutes. Add the garlic and the white part of the green onion (reserve the green parts for the garnish). Continue cooking, stirring intermittently, until the sliced onion is completely softened and just beginning to brown on the edges, another 4 minutes or so.

**5.** While the onion is cooking, in a small bowl, stir together the gochujang, 2 to 3 teaspoons gochugaru (depending on how spicy you'd like your sauce), and the sesame oil. Stir until the mixture becomes a thick paste, then stir in the sugar and soy sauce until smooth.

*(recipe continues)*

● ● ●

**6.** When the onions are done cooking, scrape the sauce into the pan and stir to combine. Slowly pour in the heavy cream, whisking constantly. Reduce the heat to low and simmer, whisking intermittently as the sauce thickens slightly and becomes rich and velvety (the whisk should leave a slight trail when dragged through the sauce), another few minutes. Taste the sauce and add salt and pepper as needed, likely a few good pinches of each if not more.

**7.** Strain the thawed noodles and cook in the boiling water for 2 minutes, stirring intermittently. Reserve one cup of the pasta water and set aside before straining the noodles.

**8.** Strain the noodles and add them to the pan with the rosé sauce. Using tongs, move them around in the sauce to thoroughly coat. Pour in a small amount of pasta water, continuing to move the noodles around, thinning the sauce to the desired consistency.

**9.** Using the tongs, transfer the noodles to a large bowl or rimmed platter and top with the crispy pork belly and the eggs, then garnish with the reserved chopped green onion and sesame seeds. Serve and enjoy. Leftover noodles may be stored in the refrigerator for up to 3 days.

So many of my treasured Korean dishes are full-on comfort foods, and this is one of them. Using leftover, or at least day-old, rice is essential when making this dish, and it needs to be cold, so a little planning ahead is needed. I add Spam because it's my favorite, and it adds saltiness, but if you want a vegetarian meal, you can easily leave it out. This is really a use-up-all-your-leftovers-clean-out-your-fridge kinda dish, so use whatever veggies or meats you have. If you find you have more of an everything-else-to-rice ratio, don't worry. For me, more is always more!

# KIMCHI FRIED RICE WITH AN EGG

### Serves 6

- 3 tablespoons toasted sesame oil, divided
- 1 (7-ounce) can Spam, finely diced
- 5 tablespoons unsalted butter, divided
- 1 carrot, peeled and finely diced
- 1 zucchini, finely diced
- ½ medium yellow onion, finely diced
- 4 medium garlic cloves, minced or grated
- 1½ cups kimchi, finely chopped
- 4 cups leftover cooked white rice
- 1 tablespoon gochujang paste or 1 tablespoon gochugaru coarse chile flakes
- 1 tablespoon soy sauce
- 1 tablespoon granulated sugar (optional)
- ½ teaspoon kosher salt, or more as needed
- Freshly ground black pepper
- 6 large eggs
- 3 green onions (white and green parts), sliced on the bias, for garnish
- 2 tablespoons chili oil, plus more as needed, for garnish (optional)

**1.** In a wok or large skillet, heat 1 tablespoon of sesame oil over medium-high heat, and cook the Spam until it's crispy, 5 to 7 minutes. Remove the Spam from the skillet and set aside.

**2.** Reduce the heat to medium and melt 2 tablespoons of butter. Add the carrot, zucchini, and onion and cook until the vegetables are just softened, 5 to 7 minutes. Add the garlic and cook until softened, another minute. Lastly, add the kimchi until it's warmed through.

**3.** Next, stir in the remaining 3 tablespoons of butter, the rice, gochujang (or gochugaru flakes for a very spicy mix!), soy sauce, 1 tablespoon of oil, the sugar if using, and the salt and stir until the butter has melted and everything is evenly distributed. Taste and season with more salt, if needed, and a few pinches of pepper.

**4.** Continue to cook until your rice reaches the desired crispiness. I like to press the mixture into the skillet and let it cook until the bottom is crispy like a traditional Korean stone bowl. Remove the rice from the stovetop while you cook the eggs.

**5.** In a separate nonstick skillet over medium heat, heat the remaining tablespoon of oil until it shimmers. Gently crack the eggs into the skillet and fry for 2 to 3 minutes, until the whites are set.

**6.** Divide the rice among 6 bowls and top each one with a fried egg and garnish with the green onions and a drizzle of the chili oil, if using.

**7.** Serve warm. Leftover fried rice may be stored in an airtight container in the refrigerator for up to 4 days.

Another of my Korean-fusion recipes, this one combines my two great loves: grilled cheese and kimchi! Cal's OBSESSED with all things cheese and pork belly, so I randomly made this recipe for him, and now he asks for it whenever we can't decide what to have for dinner. I've said it before and I'll say it again: I believe most any Korean recipe pairs well with melted cheese. If you don't have a panini press, get creative. I stack a few pots and bowls on top of my grill pan to help create perfectly crispy grill lines. When buying pork belly, look for thinly cut slices, which will resemble bacon in the package (see page 20 for more on pork belly). This cut is easily found in most Asian markets.

# CHEESY KIMCHI PORK BELLY PANINI

### Makes 1 sandwich

- ¼ teaspoon garlic powder
- ¼ teaspoon onion powder
- ¼ teaspoon gochugaru coarse chile flakes
- 4 thinly-cut pork belly slices (about 3 ounces)
- 3 tablespoons unsalted butter, softened
- 2 slices sourdough bread
- 2 ounces fresh mozzarella cheese, sliced
- 3 tablespoons kimchi

**1.** In a small bowl, combine the garlic powder, onion powder, and gochugaru and sprinkle it on all sides of the pork belly slices. In a medium skillet, over medium-high heat, add the pork belly and cook until it is cooked through and crispy, 4 to 5 minutes per side. Using tongs or a fork, transfer the cooked pork belly to a paper towel-lined plate to absorb the excess oil.

**2.** Butter one side of each slice of sourdough bread, then begin building your sandwich. Place one piece of bread, buttered side down, on your work space. Spread half the mozzarella slices evenly across the bread, then top with the cooked pork belly slices, then the kimchi, followed by another layer of mozzarella, and top with the second piece of bread, butter side up.

**3.** Preheat your panini press if you have one. If not, heat a grill pan over medium-high heat and toast the sandwich, pressing down firmly to create grill marks, 3 to 5 minutes. When the grill marks appear, using a spatula, flip the sandwich, and continue cooking until grill marks appear on the second side and the cheese starts to melt, another 3 to 5 minutes. If using a panini press, cook until grill marks appear and the cheese starts to melt.

**4.** Transfer the toasted sandwich to a cutting board, slice down the center, and enjoy! The grilled cheese is best enjoyed right away.

LET'S GET COOKING

Get ready for your new favorite Korean meal: Galbi! These marinated short ribs are a sweet and savory staple in the Cruz household. Back when I was growing up, my parents made them for dinner at least once a week, so they always bring back memories of my dad cooking them on our outdoor grill. My brother, Shane, and I would sneak out for a little taste, which my dad would call a "Scooby Snack." The marinade gets its sweetness from plum syrup and a pear puree, which mixes perfectly with the soy sauce's saltiness and gochujang's heat. Although pear puree and plum syrup are the traditional way to add sweetness to this dish (it adds a different type of sweetness than honey or sugar), if you don't have the syrup, you can forgo it. The dish is still plenty sweet. The cut of the meat is something you don't want to change, though. Look for an LA-style cut of short rib for this recipe, which is a boneless flanken cut (the short ribs are cut across the bone instead of the more common cut found in English-cut short ribs, see page 20). If you're in a hurry, you can shorten the marinade time to a few hours, but it's best to let them soak in the flavors overnight. If you're wondering why I soak the ribs in water before marinating, it's to draw out impurities (the meat becomes paler as it soaks) and I find it changes the flavor profile, making it less gamey. Galbi is kind of the Korean equivalent of a chicken wing. We eat the ribs with our hands, grizzle and all. When Cal and I first met and he did the same (a non-Korean who ate the galbi with his hands, grizzle and all), I knew we were soulmates.

# GALBI (MARINATED SHORT RIBS)

### Serves 6

**FOR THE MARINADE**

- 4 pounds Korean-style flanken-cut short ribs (see page 20)
- 1 Asian pear, peeled, cored, and roughly chopped
- 1 small white onion, roughly chopped
- 8 large garlic cloves, peeled and roughly chopped
- ½ cup soy sauce
- ½ cup rice wine vinegar
- ⅓ cup packed light brown sugar
- ¼ cup plum syrup

**1.** Put the ribs in a large bowl and fill it with cold water. Allow the ribs to sit for 10 to 20 minutes, then rinse and set aside.

**2.** Make the marinade: In a blender, combine the pear, onion, garlic, soy sauce, vinegar, brown sugar, plum syrup, ginger, oil, and gochujang and puree until smooth.

**3.** Put the rinsed ribs in a resealable bag or container with a lid, add the marinade and the green onions, seal tightly, and turn the bag or container a couple of times to cover the ribs with the marinade.

**4.** Refrigerate for at least 3 hours or up to 24 hours before cooking.

*(recipe and ingredients continue)*

1 thumb-length piece fresh ginger, peeled

3 tablespoons toasted sesame oil

4 teaspoons gochujang paste

4 green onions (white and green parts), chopped into 3-inch pieces

**5.** Once marinated, bring the ribs to room temperature (about 30 minutes out of the refrigerator). Heat a large nonstick skillet over medium-high heat (nonstick is key!) and cook the ribs for 3 to 5 minutes per side, until caramelized and crispy. If you'd like to serve the green onions as well, you may pull them from the marinade and cook them until they are slightly softened, for about 3 minutes over high heat. Discard the rest of the marinade.

**6.** Serve immediately or use the cooked galbi to make Korean Short Rib (Galbi) Breakfast Burritos (page 31).

This fragrant stew-like braise is one of my ultimate comfort foods. It's a labor of love, and the flavor profile seems unique to me. While the meat slowly cooks, the sweet and savory warming aroma wafts through the house and excites me for what is to come. When buying short ribs for this dish, you want an English-style cut, not to be confused with a flanken style used in Galbi (page 169). This Korean classic, often served for special occasions, is a little more time-intensive than some of the other recipes in this book, but it's a set-it-and-forget-it kind of dish; plus, it makes a lot, so you can freeze a good deal of it. Even though it never gets that cold in California, I still crave this stew even on hot days, so once the temp drops below 80 degrees, I pull out a quart from my freezer, allow it to thaw, and reheat it on the stove for the most comforting, delicious dinner.

# GALBI-JJIM (BRAISED BEEF SHORT RIB STEW)

### Serves 8

**FOR THE PEAR PUREE**

- 2 small Korean pears, cored and cut into 2-inch cubes
- 1 small white onion, peeled and coarsely chopped (about 1 cup)
- 4 medium green onions (white and green parts), coarsely chopped
- 8 medium garlic cloves
- ½-inch knob fresh ginger, peeled and chopped
- 2 tablespoons toasted sesame oil

**FOR THE STEW**

- 3½ pounds (2-inch pieces) English-style short ribs (see page 20)
- 2 tablespoons vegetable oil or other neutral oil
- ¼ cup granulated sugar

**1.** Make the pear puree: In a food processor combine the pears, white onion, green onions, garlic, ginger, and oil and process on high to form a smooth puree. Set aside.

**2.** Make the stew: Fill a large bowl with cold water and submerge the ribs, soaking them for 30 minutes to remove any impurities. Drain and, using a paper towel, pat dry.

**3.** Heat the oil in a large pot or Dutch oven over medium-high heat until it shimmers. Add the ribs in a single layer and cook until browned on both sides, about 3 minutes per side.

**4.** To the pot with the short ribs add the sugar, soy sauce, plum syrup, salt, pepper, and the reserved pear puree and stir. Then add the water and stock. Bring the mixture to a boil. Reduce the heat to low and simmer, partially covered, for 1 hour 30 minutes.

*(recipe and ingredients continue)*

MY FAVORITE KOREAN DISHES

¼ cup soy sauce

¼ cup Korean plum syrup

1 teaspoon kosher salt

½ teaspoon freshly ground black pepper

4 cups water

1 cup beef stock

3 large carrots, peeled and cut into 1-inch pieces

1 russet potato, peeled and cut into 1-inch pieces

6 green onions (white and green parts), cut into 2-inch pieces

1 large white onion, coarsely chopped

1 teaspoon gochugaru coarse chile flakes

3 to 4 cups cooked white rice, for serving (optional)

● ● ●

**5.** Add the carrots, potato, green onions, white onion, and the gochugaru (you can use less or more to taste) and continue to slowly simmer until the meat on the short ribs becomes tender and easily pulls off the bone and the vegetables are fork-tender, about 30 to 40 minutes longer or more. (The stew may take 2 hours total or even slightly longer depending on the size and meatiness of the ribs.)

**6.** Serve over rice, if desired, or enjoy by itself. Leftover stew may be stored in an airtight container in the refrigerator for up to 4 days. Reheat in a pot on the stovetop over medium until heated through.

# get a bite with EVERY

# *a little of*

# THING

When I was little, my mom made kimchi-jjigae all the time—however, it wasn't my favorite dish, TBH. The one thing I *did* like about it was the pieces of Spam. Growing up, we had a second fridge in the garage for all our Korean foods, where there was often a giant pot of kimchi stew. I loved Spam so much that at night I would sneak into the garage and fish out all the pieces of Spam from the stew to eat! I like to equate this dish to a Midwestern Crock-Pot meal, where you throw in what you have. Here you can use tofu instead of pork belly and ribs (although the pork fat is what makes the broth taste so good!). As an adult I have a new appreciation for this dish. Add whatever meats and veggies you like, season with Korean chile flakes, load up the kimchi, and let it stew! Eat leftovers over cooked white rice for a delicious next-day meal.

# MOM'S KIMCHI-JJIGAE (KIMCHI STEW)

*Makes 2½ quarts (10 cups)*

- 1 tablespoon toasted sesame oil, plus more as needed
- 8 ounces boneless, skinless pork belly, cut into 1-inch pieces
- 8 ounces boneless pork ribs, cut into 1-inch pieces
- ½ small head red or green cabbage, cored and chopped into 2-inch pieces (about 4 cups)
- 1 large yellow onion, chopped (about 1½ cups)
- 1 bunch green onions (white and green parts), thinly sliced (about 1 cup)
- 5 medium garlic cloves, sliced
- 1 tablespoon sesame seeds, plus more for garnish
- 1 tablespoon gochugaru coarse chile flakes
- 2 tablespoons unsalted butter
- 1 (32-ounce) jar kimchi, coarsely chopped, liquid reserved
- 1 quart water
- 1 (12-ounce) can Spam, cut into 1-inch pieces

**1.** Heat the oil in a large pot or Dutch oven over medium-high heat until it shimmers. Add the pork belly and pork ribs and cook until the meat begins to brown, using tongs to flip the pieces only when needed to prevent burning, 8 to 10 minutes. Add the cabbage, yellow onion, the green onions (reserving a tablespoon or two for garnish), and the garlic and stir to combine. Continue to cook, stirring, until the onions just become softened, 3 to 4 minutes, adding a teaspoon or two more of sesame oil as needed to prevent the vegetables sticking to the pot.

**2.** Stir in the sesame seeds and gochugaru to coat the vegetables, and cook until fragrant, 1 to 2 minutes. Next, add the butter and cook until it just begins to melt, then add the kimchi (including the liquid from the jar), the water, and the Spam (my favorite!).

**3.** Cover and cook over low heat for at least 20 minutes. For deeper flavor, cook the stew for 2 to 4 hours before serving.

**4.** To serve, transfer the stew to a large serving bowl or individual bowls and garnish with sesame seeds and the reserved green onions. The stew may be stored in the refrigerator for up to 5 days.

LET'S GET COOKING

This recipe is truly one of my favorites in the entire book. The pride I felt when I tasted these meatballs during recipe testing was unbelievable. If you're a meatball lover like me, but perhaps interested in a new twist, this recipe is for you—it comes together quickly, can feed a ton of people, and the sweet-and-spicy glaze takes the meatballs to the next level. I especially like getting my hands into the bowl and mixing and squishing the ingredients together because it's really tactile. Using my hands also helps so the meat doesn't get overworked. Forming the balls is a real hands-on task, too. It's a good job to give a partner or friend, *and* it's a fun way to get your loved ones involved in the kitchen with you.

# SWEET AND SPICY GOCHUJANG MEATBALLS

### *Makes 30 meatballs*

**FOR THE MEATBALLS**

Cooking spray or spray oil

2 tablespoons unsalted butter

2 medium carrots, peeled and finely diced (about 1 cup)

1 small zucchini, finely diced

½ medium yellow onion, finely diced (about ½ cup)

5 green onions (white and green parts separated), white parts minced; green parts cut on the bias, for garnish

4 small garlic cloves, minced (about 1 heaping tablespoon)

1¾ teaspoons kosher salt, divided

½ teaspoon freshly ground black pepper, plus more for seasoning

1 cup whole milk

¼ cup gochujang paste

1 cup plain breadcrumbs, homemade (page 24) or store-bought

2 pounds ground turkey

1 large egg, lightly whisked

1 to 2 tablespoons sesame seeds, for garnish

3 to 4 cups cooked white rice, for serving (optional)

**1.** Make the meatballs: Preheat the oven to 350°F. Spray 2 rimmed baking sheets generously with cooking spray. Set aside.

**2.** In a large skillet over medium heat, melt the butter. Add the carrots, zucchini, yellow onion, and whites of the green onion, cooking until softened, about 5 to 7 minutes.

**3.** Add the garlic, ¼ teaspoon of salt, and a few grinds of pepper, stirring to combine, and cook for another 2 to 3 minutes. Remove the cooked vegetables from the heat and let cool.

**4.** In a medium microwave-safe bowl, heat the milk in the microwave for 1 minute on high. Whisk in the gochujang until fully combined, then add the breadcrumbs and stir until moistened.

**5.** In a large bowl, combine the turkey, cooked vegetables, moistened breadcrumbs, egg, and the remaining 1½ teaspoons of salt and the ½ teaspoon of pepper. Using your hands (or a rubber spatula or wooden spoon if you prefer), mix the ingredients until just combined.

**6.** Using a heaping tablespoon (or your hands), form uniform-size balls (you should get 30). Place the meatballs an inch or two apart on the prepared baking sheets and spray the tops of the meatballs with cooking spray.

*(recipe and ingredients continue)*

**FOR THE GLAZE**

4 tablespoons (½ stick) unsalted butter

2 tablespoons gochujang paste

4 tablespoons honey

• • •

**7.** Bake the meatballs until browned on the bottoms, about 25 minutes, then, using a spatula or tongs, very gently flip them, and cook until they are evenly browned and cooked through inside, another 15 minutes or so. Remove the meatballs from the oven, adjust a rack to 6 inches below the broiler, and turn the broiler to high.

**8.** Make the glaze: In a small pot over medium-low heat, melt the butter. Once the butter has melted, remove the pot from heat and whisk in the gochujang and honey.

**9.** Brush each cooked meatball all over with the glaze and broil until the glaze just starts to bubble, but be careful, it burns very quickly. You'll only want to broil them for 2 to 3 minutes.

**10.** To serve, garnish with the remaining green onions, the sesame seeds, and a side of cooked white rice, if using. Enjoy! Leftover meatballs may be stored in the refrigerator for up to 4 days and reheated, covered with foil, in a 300°F oven for about 10 minutes, or until heated through.

While developing recipes for this book, I'll never forget the joy on my team's faces as they bit into this juicy chicken sandwich. It is hands-down their favorite recipe. It is one of my very favorites in the book, too, not only because I love how this sandwich tastes—brushing the meat with a sweet and spicy gochujang glaze adds a fun twist to a traditional fried chicken sandwich and the Asian pear slaw adds a refreshing bite—but I am so happy when the people I adore love what I make.

# KOREAN FRIED CHICKEN SANDWICH WITH ASIAN PEAR SLAW

*Makes 4 sandwiches*

**FOR THE SAUCE**

4 tablespoons (½ stick) unsalted butter
2 medium garlic cloves, minced
⅓ cup honey
¼ cup gochujang paste

**FOR THE SLAW**

2 tablespoons Kewpie mayonnaise or other Japanese mayonnaise
1 tablespoon soy sauce
1 tablespoon mirin
1 teaspoon granulated sugar
Kosher salt
Freshly ground black pepper
1 small Korean pear, peeled and cut into thin strips (about 1 heaping cup)
½ cup finely shredded cabbage
2 green onions (white and green parts), finely chopped

**FOR THE CHICKEN**

½ cup all-purpose flour
½ teaspoon kosher salt, divided
¼ teaspoon garlic powder

**1.** Make the sauce: In a small pot over medium heat, melt the butter. Add the garlic and cook, stirring until the garlic becomes fragrant, 1 to 2 minutes. Reduce the heat to low and whisk in the honey and gochujang until smooth. Remove from the heat and set aside.

**2.** Make the slaw: In a medium bowl, whisk together the mayonnaise, soy sauce, mirin, sugar, a few generous pinches of salt to taste, and a few pinches of pepper. Taste the dressing and adjust the seasonings as needed. Toss in the pear, cabbage, and green onions, and, using a rubber spatula, fold the ingredients until the cabbage and pear are thoroughly coated with the dressing. Set aside.

**3.** Make the chicken: Prepare the breading stations using 3 wide, shallow rimmed bowls. In the first bowl, whisk together the flour, ¼ teaspoon of salt, the garlic powder, onion powder, and a few pinches of pepper. In the second bowl, crack the eggs and whisk well. In the third bowl, combine the panko with the remaining ¼ teaspoon of salt and a few pinches of pepper.

**4.** With one hand (we'll call this your dry hand), dip a piece of chicken into the flour, fully coating it, then switch the chicken to your other hand (we'll call this your wet hand), dip the flour-coated thigh in the whisked egg, fully coating it again, then dip the thigh in the third dish with the

*(recipe and ingredients continue)*

MY FAVORITE KOREAN DISHES    **181**

¼ teaspoon onion powder

Freshly ground black pepper

2 large eggs

½ cup panko breadcrumbs

4 boneless, skinless chicken thighs (about 1½ pounds), patted dry with a paper towel

1 quart vegetable oil or other high-heat neutral oil, for frying

4 tablespoons (½ stick) unsalted butter, softened

4 seeded brioche or hamburger buns

• • •

panko, pressing it to adhere the coating over the entire thigh. Using your dry hand, put the breaded thigh on a plate or baking sheet and repeat the coating procedure with the remaining thighs, beginning with the wet hand and ending with your dry hand.

**5.** To fry the chicken, pour the oil into a large saucepan (you want the oil to be about a ½-high for a shallow fry) and heat to 350°F (see page 23 for more on frying). Using tongs or a spider, lower the chicken into the oil and fry until the coating is golden brown and the thighs are cooked through, about 8 minutes per side. Transfer the cooked chicken to a clean plate or baking sheet.

**6.** If the glaze is no longer smooth and brushable, heat it for 1 to 2 minutes, then, using a basting brush, coat the fried chicken thighs all over with the glaze.

**7.** Butter the buns, and if desired, toast them in a skillet for 1 to 2 minutes on the stovetop.

**8.** Serve the fried glazed chicken thigh on a bun topped with a spoonful of slaw. Enjoy! These sandwiches are best eaten right away.

LET'S GET COOKING

Street sandwiches are HUGE in Korea. You can get many types, including bulgogi and the well-known gilgeori toast, an egg and cabbage sandwich. When I'm roaming the streets of Korea, I look forward to the smell of these deliciously fresh sandwiches wafting in the air. In general, I am not a ham and cheese girl, but there's something about the sweet bread and spicy mayo that makes this combo special and one I love.

# KOREAN STREET-STYLE HAM AND CHEESE SANDWICHES WITH SWEET SRIRACHA MAYO

*Make 4 sandwiches*

- 4 tablespoons (½ stick) unsalted butter, divided
- 8 slices 1½-inch-thick brioche bread, or your white bread of choice
- 1 batch Sweet Sriracha Mayo (page 24)
- ½ pound (about 12 slices) sliced deli ham
- ½ pound (about 12 slices) sliced deli Swiss cheese

1. In a large skillet over medium heat, melt 1 tablespoon of butter. Add two slices of bread and toast until golden brown, about 2 minutes on each side. Remove the toasted bread and repeat with the remaining slices, adding more butter as needed.

2. Assemble the sandwiches: Lay all the toasted bread slices on a surface, toasted side down. Spread the sriracha mayo on the nontoasted side of each slice. On half of the slices, layer equal pieces ham and cheese. Top each with another slice of bread, mayo-side down, to form the sandwiches.

3. Heat the skillet used to toast the bread over medium heat again. Add one sandwich to the skillet and let it cook until the cheese begins to melt and the bread gets crispy, about 2 minutes. For faster melting, add a few drops of water to the skillet and cover it with a lid to create steam. Let the sandwich steam for 1 minute. Then remove the lid, flip the sandwich, and toast the other side, another 1 to 2 minutes.

4. Once both sides are golden and the cheese has fully melted, remove the sandwich from the skillet. Repeat the cooking process with the remaining sandwiches.

5. To serve, slice in half or serve whole, as is often done in Korea. The sandwiches are best eaten right away.

I'm not sure how this dish was born. It's not Korean corn cheese, for those familiar with the popular side, the cheesy, bubbly corn dish often served at Korean barbecue restaurants—and it's not really cornbread, either. It's some type of deliciously sweet cornbready thing that I'm calling a casserole in honor of my favorite Midwesterners. The edges are cooked and light, and the center is rich and gooey. You can spoon it up like you would a traditional corn hot dish, or try it as a side to chili or scoop it up with chips. Let me know what you think.

# KOREAN CHEESY CORN CASSEROLE

### Serves 6

- 1 (12-ounce) bag cornbread mix (about 2¼ cups)
- 1 (12-ounce) can evaporated milk
- ½ cup (1 stick) unsalted butter, melted
- ¼ cup honey, plus more for drizzling
- 1 large egg
- 1 teaspoon kosher salt
- 1 (15.25-ounce) can sweet corn, drained
- 2 cups (8 ounces) shredded mozzarella cheese, divided
- A small bowl of potato chips, for serving (optional)

**1.** Preheat the oven to 350°F.

**2.** In an 8-inch square pan or casserole dish, pour in the cornbread mix. Add the milk, butter, honey, egg, and salt and whisk until combined. Using a rubber spatula, fold in the corn and 1 cup of mozzarella until thoroughly combined and no dry bits are left. Spread the mixture evenly in the pan.

**3.** Sprinkle the remaining cup of mozzarella over the cornbread batter, cover with foil, and bake for 45 minutes, then uncover and bake until the cheese has melted and the center doesn't shake in the middle, about another 10 to 15 minutes. It will be somewhat gooey but it shouldn't be raw.

**4.** When the casserole is finished baking, drizzle with honey and enjoy with or without chips! Leftover casserole may be stored in the refrigerator for up to 3 days. To reheat, cover with foil and bake in an oven preheated to 350°F until heated through, about 10 minutes.

# Unbothered and Cozy WEEK MEALS

No matter how hot it might be on any given LA day, I'm a self-proclaimed "soup girl" who never says no to a bowl of soup. Because I'm an obsessive meal-prepper, I often have a quart of something brothy in the freezer that I can defrost to satisfy my soup cravings. Having food ready in the fridge after a long day of vlogging is a form of self-care for me and SO GOOD. When I'm cooking or prepping weeknight dinners, I channel my inner Rachael Ray to create quick and easy meals. If I can get dinner on the table within 30 minutes it's a win in my book. Although I strive for fast, I never compromise on flavor and work hard to keep things tasting interesting—and always with a cozy spin. I eat most of my meals at home versus dining out (and often in my pjs on the couch), and I love to re-create comfort foods from my favorite restaurants. Many recipes in this chapter were inspired by dishes I've enjoyed while traveling—like the Hawaiian Garlic Shrimp on page 193. I hope you enjoy this collection of my favorite cozy, no-fuss meals that come together quickly—even after a long day.

- Hawaiian Garlic Shrimp  193
- Mango and Brie Cheesy Quesadillas  195
- Sweet Chili Fried Salmon Bites with Hot Honey Brussels Sprouts  196
- Roasted Japanese Sweet Potato Soup with Garlicky Croutons  199
- Cozy Butternut Squash Soup  201
- Buffalo Chicken–Stuffed Sweet Potatoes  204
- Crispy Rice Salad  207
- The Best Turkey Burger You'll Ever Have  208
- Cruz Family's Famous Chicken Tenders  213
- Caramelized Onion Chicken with Mushrooms  215
- "Better Than That Furniture Store" Swedish Meatballs  219
- Comforting Rice Cooker Ginger Garlic Chicken  221
- Vietnamese Shaking Beef Bowls (Bò Lúc Lắc)  225
- Honey Peanut Chicken Bowl  226
- Honey Mustard–Glazed Salmon with Garlic Parmesan Roasted Potatoes  229
- Liquid Gold Lemony Shrimp Linguine  230
- Vodka Sauce Pasta with Crispy Chicken  233
- Garlic Lovers Shrimp & Noods  235
- Coconut Curry Shrimp & Chicken Bowl  239
- Air Fryer Teriyaki Drumsticks  240

If you watch my vlogs, you know I love nothing more than going on a trip. I love visiting Hawaii—not only for the beaches, views, and hospitality—but also the local dishes that capture the essence of the islands. I know it's a little controversial as to who has the best garlic shrimp in Hawaii (there's an ongoing battle for the top spot on the island), but Giovanni's Shrimp Truck is always a must-stop for me. It is one of the most iconic food trucks in the 50th state. To me, their garlic shrimp is UNBELIEVABLE. Bursting with flavor, it has just the right amount of garlic and butter and has me salivating at the thought of it. The flavors are so unforgettable that when I'm back home, I find myself craving that same taste. After a lot of experimenting, I've come up with my version of Givoanni's famous garlic shrimp. It's my way of bringing a piece of Hawaii home. And yes, there is no mistake in this recipe, I *want* you to eat these shrimp with the shells on as they do in Hawaii and many parts of the world. The shells add to the flavor and texture, and leaving them on also helps the shrimp not overcook. If you've never tried them, please do. If it's not your thing, go ahead and peel them, I promise I won't judge you!

# HAWAIIAN GARLIC SHRIMP

### Serves 4

- 2 pounds jumbo shrimp, heads-off and shell-on
- ½ cup all-purpose flour
- ½ cup potato starch
- 1 teaspoon kosher salt, divided
- 1 cup (2 sticks) unsalted butter
- 10 to 12 medium garlic cloves, minced or grated
- Freshly ground black pepper
- 2 cups vegetable oil or other high-heat neutral oil, for frying, plus more as needed
- 3 to 4 cups cooked white rice, for serving
- 4 lemon wedges, for serving

**1.** Rinse the shrimp, and then, using kitchen shears, cut into the back of each shrimp and remove the vein (the dark line running down the back of the shrimp) while leaving the shell intact. You can use a paring knife, toothpick, or even your finger to slide the vein out. Rinse the shrimp again and, using a paper towel, dry the shrimp well.

**2.** In a medium bowl, whisk together the flour, potato starch, and ½ teaspoon of salt.

**3.** Put the shrimp in the flour/starch mixture and toss to evenly coat, getting the flour into all the crevices. Dust off any excess coating.

**4.** In a large saucepan over medium-high, melt the butter, then add the garlic, the remaining ½ teaspoon of salt, and a few pinches of pepper. Stir and cook the garlic for 30 seconds. Transfer the garlic butter to the bowl you'll be using to serve the shrimp. Wipe out the saucepan if any garlic remains because you are going to heat the oil in the same pan.

*(recipe continues)*

WEEKNIGHT MEALS

• • •

**5.** Now pour the oil into the saucepan. Your oil should be about ¼-inch deep in the pan. If it's not, add more. Heat the oil until it reaches 350°F on a candy thermometer (or see page 23 on how to test the oil without a thermometer). Line a plate with paper towels and set aside.

**6.** When the oil is hot, using a spider, slotted spoon, or tongs, lower the shrimp into the oil in a single layer. Do not overcrowd the pan. Work in batches if you need to.

**7.** Fry the shrimp until it starts to turn pink, 2 minutes, then, using tongs or a fork, turn each shrimp to cook on the other side until it is pink for another 2 minutes. You want to work quickly as shrimp can overcook in seconds. Transfer the shrimp to the prepared plate.

**8.** While the shrimp are still hot, put them in the bowl with the garlic butter and toss the shrimp until coated with the butter.

**9.** Serve over white rice with a lemon wedge on the side. I recommend pouring any excess butter over the rice—it makes a delicious sauce. Leftover shrimp may be refrigerated in an airtight container for up to 2 days. Eat them cold right out of the fridge.

Years ago, I stopped at a restaurant called Maracas in Palm Springs where I first tried the combination of brie and mango in a quesadilla. It's the only place I've ever seen those two things together between tortillas, and let me tell you, it was memorable. As I like to do, I re-created the recipe at home with my own twist of additional mozzarella for extra cheesiness. This recipe reminds me of a cheese board in a quesadilla. I wouldn't usually pair these ingredients together, but I promise it will leave you wanting more!

# MANGO AND BRIE CHEESY QUESADILLAS

### Serves 4

- 4 tablespoons (½ stick) unsalted butter, divided
- 6 to 8 (8- to 10-inch) flour tortillas
- 2 cups (8 ounces) shredded mozzarella cheese
- 1 mango, peeled and sliced into thin strips
- 4 ounces brie cheese, cubed (about 1 cup)
- Kosher salt and freshly black pepper, for seasoning
- ½ cup salsa of choice, for serving

1. Preheat the oven to 300°F.

2. In a large skillet, over medium heat, melt 1 to 2 teaspoons of butter.

3. Working with one tortilla at a time, lay one in the skillet to warm and crisp up some, 1 to 2 minutes.

4. Using tongs, flip the tortilla and sprinkle half of the tortilla (you are going to fold it in half) with an even layer of mozzarella, then add a few mango slices in a single layer and some cubes of brie sporadically around the same half tortilla. Finish with a few pinches of salt and pepper. Fold the tortilla in half.

5. Using a spatula, lift the tortilla and add another 1 to 2 teaspoons of butter to the saucepan to melt and flip the tortilla over, cooking until the cheese has melted and the tortillas are crisp and golden, 2 to 3 minutes. Transfer the cooked quesadilla to a rimmed baking sheet and put it in the oven to keep warm while you cook the rest of the quesadillas. Repeat the quesadilla-making process until all the ingredients are used.

6. Remove the warm quesadillas from the oven, slice each one into 4 triangles, and serve with your favorite salsa. These quesadillas are best eaten right away.

Sweet chili sauce is the secret ingredient to this one-pan weeknight dinner (although it's fancy enough to serve at a dinner party!). I always keep a bottle of this tangy, savory yet sweet Thai condiment, which is often served with spring rolls, in my fridge because it goes great with many things, including fish. It's like a premade glaze in a bottle. Shaving the Brussels sprouts is another time-saver that cuts down on the cooking time, too. If you're interested in making your own Hot Honey, check out page 24, but if you don't have the time or the desire to make your own, store-bought works just as well. One of my favorite small businesses to support—and one featured in my 2020 Vlogmas—is AR's Hot Southern Honey. I highly recommend trying it!

# SWEET CHILI FRIED SALMON BITES WITH HOT HONEY BRUSSELS SPROUTS

*Serves 2*

**FOR THE SALMON**

- ¼ cup Thai sweet chili sauce
- 2 medium garlic cloves, minced or grated
- 2 teaspoons grated fresh ginger
- 2 teaspoons toasted sesame oil
- ½ teaspoon kosher salt
- ⅛ teaspoon freshly ground black pepper
- 1 pound skinless center-cut salmon fillet, rinsed, patted dry, and cut into ½-inch cubes

**FOR THE BRUSSELS SPROUTS**

- 2 tablespoons extra-virgin olive oil
- 8 ounces Brussels sprouts, shaved (about 2 cups)
- 1 tablespoon Hot Honey (page 24) or store-bought
- ½ teaspoon kosher salt
- ⅛ teaspoon freshly ground black pepper

1. Make the salmon: In a medium bowl, stir together the sweet chili sauce, garlic, ginger, sesame oil, salt, and pepper. Add the salmon to the mixture, gently tossing to evenly coat. Let the salmon marinate in the fridge for 10 to 15 minutes.

2. Preheat a large, nonstick skillet over medium heat until a drop of water sizzles in it. Add the marinated salmon cubes, discarding the extra marinade, and cook on each side until browned and crispy, 2 to 3 minutes per side for medium-rare. Once cooked, using tongs or a spatula, transfer the salmon to a plate and set aside.

3. Make the Brussels sprouts: In the same pan, reduce the heat to low and heat the olive oil until it shimmers. Add the shaved sprouts in a single layer, spreading them out across the bottom of the pan. Cover with a lid and cook until the Brussels begin to char, 3 to 5 minutes. Remove the lid, stir, and season with the honey, salt, and pepper. Cook until the sprouts are caramelized and tender, an additional 2 to 3 minutes.

4. Serve the Brussels warm with the cooked salmon cubes. The salmon and Brussels sprouts are best eaten right after they are cooked.

You probably know by now that when I cook, I go big: big flavors, big textures, and big portions. This recipe makes—yep, you guessed it—a big pot of hearty soup that is perfect for colder weather. The pale yellow flesh of Japanese sweet potatoes, which have a reddish-purple skin, is drier and creamier than orange sweet potatoes, and when roasted has an almost chestnut-like flavor. If you don't see these cousins of the orange-fleshed variety in your produce section, try an Asian market. It's worth the hunt—I promise. And the soup itself is super easy. It's really just two ingredients: sweet potatoes and broth, plus some seasoning and cream if you like things a little more decadent. The key to the big flavor here is the oil, infused with garlic for drizzling on your soup, topped by a handful of crunchy, garlicky croutons. After one spoonful, you'll give yourself a BIG thank you.

# ROASTED JAPANESE SWEET POTATO SOUP WITH GARLICKY CROUTONS

## Serves 6 to 8

**FOR THE SOUP**

4 Japanese sweet potatoes (white sweet potatoes) or regular sweet potatoes (4 to 4½ pounds)

1 cup extra-virgin olive oil

6 large garlic cloves

6 to 8 cups chicken broth

1 teaspoon kosher salt, plus more for seasoning

Freshly ground black pepper

¼ cup heavy cream

3 slices crispy cooked bacon, crumbled, for garnish

**FOR THE GARLIC BREAD CROUTONS**

3 tablespoons extra-virgin olive oil

4 slices thickly cut sourdough bread, cut into bite-size cubes

**1.** Preheat the oven to 425°F. Cover a rimmed baking sheet with foil.

**2.** Make the soup: Wash and dry the sweet potatoes. Pierce them several times with a fork. Place the sweet potatoes on the prepared baking sheet and roast until they are soft when pierced with a fork, 45 minutes to 1 hour. Remove the potatoes from the oven and allow them to cool. Once cool, peel off the skin and scoop out the flesh into a bowl. Set aside.

**3.** While the potatoes are cooling, make the oil: In a small pot over the lowest heat, combine the olive oil and garlic and cover, cooking until the garlic becomes fork-tender, 15 to 30 minutes, depending on the size of your garlic cloves. You are infusing the oil with the flavor of the garlic. You are not boiling the oil, just bringing it to the gentlest simmer possible with very slow bubbles. When the oil is done simmering, transfer the oil and garlic to a heatproof jar with a lid. (I sometimes like to add a spoonful of Italian seasoning to the oil for an herby flavor.)

*(recipe and ingredients continue)*

3 medium garlic cloves, minced

1 teaspoon dried Italian seasoning, plus more for garnish

Kosher salt

Freshly ground black pepper

**4.** Make the croutons: Heat the olive oil in a large saucepan over medium-high heat until it shimmers. Once the oil is hot, add the bread cubes and toast them, stirring constantly, until they just start to toast the slightest bit on one side, 2 to 3 minutes.

**5.** Reduce the heat to medium low and add the garlic, Italian seasoning, and 2 to 3 pinches each of salt and pepper. Stir to evenly coat the bread cubes. Continue toasting and flipping the croutons until they are golden and crispy on all sides, another 2 to 5 minutes. Remove from the heat and set aside.

**6.** In a large soup pot or Dutch oven, over medium-high heat, bring the chicken broth to a boil. Add the salt and a few pinches of pepper. Turn off the heat and add the roasted sweet potato flesh. Using an immersion blender, blend the soup until smooth. If you don't have an immersion blender, carefully transfer the soup in batches to a blender and process until smooth, then return the soup to the pot. Once blended, add the heavy cream and simmer over low heat for 30 minutes to allow the flavors to meld together. Taste the soup and add more seasoning if needed.

**7.** To serve, ladle the soup into bowls and top with the garlicky croutons, the crumbled bacon, and a drizzle of the garlic-infused oil. The soup may be stored in an airtight container in the refrigerator for up to 4 days. Reheat the soup on the stovetop over medium heat until warmed through. The garlic oil should be stored in the refrigerator, too, and will last up to 3 weeks.

### Remi's Recommendations

If you don't have chicken broth, you can make it using bouillon. For every cup of broth, substitute one teaspoon of bouillon dissolved into one cup of boiling water.

In my opinion there's nothing better than a big, cozy bowl of soup you can dip a grilled cheese sandwich into. It's my perfect cold-weather food. (Funnily enough, I also love cold weather. Sometimes I'm really not sure why I live in LA.) As soon as the weather cools the teeniest bit here, I'm ready for soup szn. I swear I could make soup every day, and Cal, who is usually not a soup person, is slowly being coaxed into liking soup because of how much I make it for us. You can easily make this soup vegan by omitting the cream and butter (or replacing it with a nondairy option) and using vegetable stock instead of chicken stock. It freezes well, too. Since butternut squash is available all year, you can really make this any time, and I do! Consider buying peeled, cubed squash for an easy shortcut.

# Cozy Butternut Squash Soup

### Serves 6 to 8

- 6 cups butternut squash, cut into 1-inch cubes (from 2 medium uncut squash equaling about 3½ pounds; if you are buying peeled, cubed squash, you'll need 2¾ pounds cubed squash)
- 2 tablespoons extra-virgin olive oil
- 1½ to 2 teaspoons kosher salt, plus more for seasoning
- ½ teaspoon freshly ground pepper, plus more for seasoning
- 3 tablespoons unsalted butter
- 1 large yellow onion, diced (about 2 cups)
- 1 leek, chopped (about ½ cup)
- 3 large garlic cloves, minced or grated
- 4 cups chicken stock
- 2 cups water, plus more as needed
- ½ cup heavy cream, plus more for drizzling
- ¼ cup nutritional yeast (optional)
- ½ teaspoon crushed red pepper flakes, plus more for garnish
- 1 tablespoon chopped fresh sage leaves, plus a few left whole for garnish
- 1 tablespoon fresh thyme leaves, plus more for garnish

**1.** Preheat the oven to 350°F.

**2.** Put the squash on a baking sheet and drizzle with the olive oil, then season with a few pinches of salt and black pepper and toss to coat. Bake the squash cubes until they are fork-tender, about 1 hour.

**3.** In a large soup pot or Dutch oven over low heat, melt the butter. Add the onion and leek and cook, stirring often, until they are translucent, 6 to 8 minutes. Add the garlic and cook until fragrant, another 1 to 2 minutes.

**4.** Add the stock and water, stirring to release any browning from the bottom of the pot, and increase the heat to high. Add the roasted squash, bring the stock to a boil, then reduce the heat to low and simmer for 5 minutes, stirring if needed. Remove the pot from the heat.

**5.** Using an immersion blender, blend the soup until smooth. If you don't have an immersion blender, carefully transfer the soup in batches to a blender and process until smooth, then return the soup to the pot. Once blended, add the heavy cream and more water, if needed, to achieve your desired consistency. Stir in the nutritional yeast, if using, and the remaining 1½ to 2 teaspoons salt, the ½ teaspoon black pepper,

*(recipe continues)*

WEEKNIGHT MEALS

the red pepper flakes, sage, and thyme. Taste and adjust the seasonings as needed. Simmer the soup over low heat for 15 minutes, stirring occasionally.

**6.** Serve warm, with a drizzle of cream and a sprinkle of red pepper flakes, sage leaves, and thyme leaves. The soup may be stored in an airtight container in the refrigerator for up to 4 days. Reheat the soup on the stovetop over medium heat until warmed through.

Years ago, when I started a health journey, this recipe helped transition my taste buds into liking better-for-you ingredients. It's a straightforward recipe that's a cinch to make in bulk—I can get into meal prep as it makes my life easier when editing my videos or having super busy days. For breakfast, I like making a few Hot Girl Coconut Chia Puddings (page 49) or Galaxy Brownie Overnight Oats (page 51) to have in the fridge. And for dinner, these stuffed sweet potatoes are it! They hit all the things for me: protein, carbs, deliciousness—and they can be made up to three days ahead and reheated in the microwave in minutes (and obviously they can be reheated in the oven, too, it just takes a little longer). Of course you can make and eat these the same day as well. Whether you eat 'em now or later, this recipe makes sweet potatoes next level.

# BUFFALO CHICKEN-STUFFED SWEET POTATOES

### Serves 4

- 4 large sweet potatoes
- 2 cups shredded meat from a rotisserie chicken (about three quarters of a chicken)
- 1½ cups shredded mozzarella cheese, divided
- ⅓ cup plus 2 tablespoons Buffalo sauce (I prefer Frank's RedHot Buffalo Wings Sauce)
- ¼ teaspoon garlic powder
- ¼ teaspoon onion powder
- Kosher salt
- Freshly ground black pepper
- 1 teaspoon dried parsley
- 1 tablespoon melted unsalted butter or extra-virgin olive oil

**1.** Preheat the oven to 425°F.

**2.** Wash and dry the sweet potatoes thoroughly. Using a fork, poke several holes around each potato to allow steam to escape while they bake. Place the sweet potatoes on a rimmed baking sheet and bake until they are fork-tender, 45 to 60 minutes, depending on the size of your potatoes. Remove them from the oven and let them cool to the touch, 15 to 20 minutes

**3.** While the sweet potatoes bake, in a large bowl, combine the shredded chicken, 1 cup of mozzarella, the ⅓ cup Buffalo sauce, the garlic powder, onion powder, 2 to 3 pinches each of salt and pepper, and the parsley. Stir until everything is well combined. Set aside.

**4.** Slice each baked sweet potato lengthwise down the middle, being careful not to cut all the way through. Into a medium bowl, carefully scoop out the insides of the potatoes to create a pocket for the filling. To the potatoes in the bowl add the butter, the remaining

2 tablespoons Buffalo sauce, and sprinkle with ½ teaspoon salt and a few pinches of pepper and mash the potatoes to create a fluffy texture. Add the potato mixture to the reserved chicken mixture and fold to combine.

**5.** Position an oven rack 5 to 6 inches from the broiler and preheat the broiler to high.

**6.** Stuff the sweet potatoes with the Buffalo chicken mixture, piling it up, stuffing the potatoes high. Place the stuffed potatoes back on the baking sheet and top with the remaining ½ cup of mozzarella, dividing it evenly between the four potatoes. Broil the potatoes for 2 to 3 minutes, until the cheese has melted and is bubbly.

**7.** Remove the potatoes from the oven and serve hot. Stuffed potatoes can be made up to 3 days ahead and stored in an airtight container in the refrigerator. Reheat the potatoes in the microwave on high until heated through, 2 to 3 minutes.

Here's the thing: If I'm having a salad, it needs to be fun, interesting, and have lots of different crunchy elements. This crispy rice salad absolutely checks all those boxes for me, and it has quickly become one of my favorite ways to enjoy salad. You can't go wrong with crispy rice when paired with crunchy fresh vegetables and a zingy dressing. I guarantee this will be a hit, whether it's for you or your whole crew!

# CRISPY RICE SALAD

### Serves 4 to 6

1½ cups leftover cooked rice

2 tablespoons extra-virgin olive oil

1 small (8 ounces) head romaine lettuce, chopped

1 Persian cucumber, sliced into rounds

½ to ¾ cup cherry tomatoes (about ½ pint), sliced into thirds

½ small red onion, thinly sliced (about ½ cup)

¼ cup fresh mint leaves, chopped

2 lime wedges, for serving

**FOR THE DRESSING**

¼ cup avocado or safflower oil

2 tablespoons mirin

2 tablespoons soy sauce

1 tablespoon honey

2 medium garlic cloves, minced or grated

Kosher salt

Freshly ground black pepper

**1.** Preheat the oven to 400°F. Line a rimmed baking sheet with foil.

**2.** Using your hands, spread the rice, breaking up any clumps, into a single-layer over the prepared baking sheet. Drizzle with the olive oil and toss to coat, making sure the rice is well coated, then spread it out again in a single layer. Bake until the rice is crispy and golden, about 1 hour.

**3.** Make the dressing: In a small bowl, whisk together the oil, mirin, soy sauce, honey, garlic, and 1 to 2 pinches each of salt and pepper. Taste and adjust the seasoning as needed.

**4.** Assemble the salad: In a large salad bowl, combine the romaine, cucumber, tomatoes, onion, and mint. Drizzle a couple tablespoons of the dressing over the salad and toss to coat. Top with the crispy rice, adding more dressing as needed, and toss again. Add a squeeze of lime, if using, for extra freshness. This salad is best eaten right away.

This is hands-down the best turkey burger recipe I've ever had, and... it was the first thing my husband, Cal, cooked for me when we first started dating. But I promise it's not just the best because Cal wooed me with it. It's also packed with loads of flavor, plus a secret unexpected ingredient—zucchini—which keeps the meat extra juicy. I like grating the zucchini extra-fine for this recipe (the small holes on a cheese grater work well). Whether you serve it on a bun with your favorite toppings (I like to stir together ketchup, mayo, and chopped pickles or relish for an In-N-Out spread dupe) or as a salad topper, these burgers are a must-try. You can even use this meat mixture to make meatballs!

# THE BEST TURKEY BURGER YOU'LL EVER HAVE

### Makes 4 burgers

2½ teaspoons kosher salt, divided

2 medium zucchini, finely grated (about 2½ cups)

2 pounds ground turkey

½ cup grated Parmesan cheese

2 medium shallots, minced (about ⅓ cup)

1 large egg, lightly whisked

1 teaspoon Italian seasoning

½ teaspoon garlic powder

½ teaspoon crushed red pepper flakes (optional)

¼ teaspoon freshly ground black pepper

Cooking spray

4 burger buns

4 pieces lettuce, for serving

4 slices tomato, for serving

Ketchup, mayonnaise, and chopped pickles or relish, for serving

**1.** In a large bowl, sprinkle 2 teaspoons of salt over the zucchini and lightly toss. Let the salt do its magic on the zucchini (to draw the moisture out), for 15 to 20 minutes.

**2.** After the zucchini has rested with the salt, transfer it to a strainer to rinse off any excess salt. Then, using your hands (or you can also put the zucchini in a kitchen towel), squeeze out as much of any remaining water as possible.

**3.** Rinse and dry the large bowl you used for salting the zucchini and in it, combine the squeezed zucchini, turkey, Parmesan, shallots, egg, Italian seasoning, garlic powder, red pepper flakes, if using, the remaining ½ teaspoon of salt, and the black pepper.

**4.** Using your hands or a large spoon, mix all the ingredients until well combined and form the meat mixture into 4 equal patties.

**5.** Coat a large skillet with cooking spray and set it over medium-high heat to preheat (if a sprinkle of water sizzles immediately in the pan, it's ready!). Cook the patties until golden brown and the internal temperature reaches at least 160°F, 4 to 5 minutes per side.

**6.** Serve the turkey burgers on a bun with lettuce, tomato, and a mix of ketchup, mayonnaise, and chopped pickles, or on top of a salad for a lighter option. The burgers are best eaten right after cooking. Enjoy.

If you watched my vlogs in 2013 (back when I was still in high school and just starting out), you might remember a chaotic episode of my best friend Kaylee and me making an absolute mess in my parents' kitchen. We were craving chicken tenders, but wanted to teach ourselves how to make them at home. We ended up developing this recipe, which includes a special seasoning mix for sprinkling on the tenders *after* they are cooked, that quickly became a Cruz family staple. I have to give little Rem and Kay a pat on the back for thinking of adding sugar to the mix because the touch of sweetness makes these tenders downright addictive. I like serving these juicy, crispy pieces of chicken with homemade french fries for a comforting, fully-fried meal.

# CRUZ FAMILY'S FAMOUS CHICKEN TENDERS

## Serves 4

- 2 teaspoons granulated sugar, divided
- 1½ teaspoons garlic powder, divided
- 1½ teaspoons onion powder, divided
- 1½ teaspoons paprika, divided
- 1 teaspoon kosher salt, divided, plus more for seasoning
- 1 cup all-purpose flour
- 2 large eggs
- 2 cups breadcrumbs, homemade (page 24) or store-bought
- ½ teaspoon freshly ground black pepper
- 1 pound chicken tenderloins, patted dry and seasoned with salt and pepper
- 1 quart vegetable oil or other high-heat neutral oil, for frying
- Your favorite dipping sauces, for serving

**1.** Make the seasoning for sprinkling on the chicken *after* frying: In a small bowl, stir together 1 teaspoon of sugar, and ½ teaspoon each of garlic powder, onion powder, paprika, and salt. Set aside.

**2.** Next, set up your breading stations using 3 shallow bowls. In one, combine the flour with the remaining 1 teaspoon of sugar and the remaining 1 teaspoon of paprika. In a second bowl, lightly whisk the eggs until frothy. In the third bowl, combine the breadcrumbs with the remaining 1 teaspoon each of garlic and onion powder, and the remaining ½ teaspoon of salt, and the pepper, stirring to combine.

**3.** With one hand, which we'll call your dry hand, place a couple of tenders in the flour and dredge them to coat, shaking off any excess. Using your other hand, now your "wet" hand, bathe the tenders in the egg mixture, fully coating them, then transfer the egg-coated tenders to the breadcrumb bowl. Now using your dry hand, sprinkle the chicken with some breadcrumbs and then toss them in the mixture, pressing the breadcrumbs to fully adhere, until the tenders are coated. Transfer the breaded tenders to a large plate or sheet pan and continue the process until all the tenderloins are coated.

*(recipe continues)*

• • •

**4.** In a large skillet over medium-high heat, pour in the vegetable oil (you should have about ½-inch of oil in the skillet for a shallow fry, see page 23 for more on frying) and heat to 350°F. Working in small batches, transfer the breaded chicken to the oil and fry until golden brown, flipping halfway through, 4 to 5 minutes per side. Transfer the fried tenders to a paper towel–lined plate and sprinkle with the prepared seasoning mixture to taste. Serve with your favorite dipping sauces.

**5.** Leftover chicken tenders may be stored in an airtight container in the refrigerator for up to 4 days. To reheat the tenders, place them on a baking sheet and warm in an oven preheated to 350°F until heated through, about 10 minutes. An air fryer works great for reheating tenders, too!

I'm a firm believer that caramelized onions make everything better. The sweet and salty flavors give depth to anything you add them to (check out my Caramelized Onion Dip, page 67). This dish is easy, comforting, and quick to make, but tastes like it took you all day. It's just a few ingredients, including chicken breasts, mushrooms, and onion. Serve it with rice, pasta, or roasted potatoes and some mixed greens for freshness. I can guarantee whoever you make this for will absolutely be blown away!

# CARAMELIZED ONION CHICKEN WITH MUSHROOMS

### Serves 4

- 4 boneless, skinless chicken breasts
- ½ teaspoon kosher salt, plus more for seasoning
- ¼ teaspoon freshly ground black pepper, plus more for seasoning
- 1 tablespoon extra-virgin olive oil
- 4 tablespoons (½ stick) unsalted butter, divided
- 1 large white onion, thinly sliced
- 1 cup white button mushrooms, sliced (about 8 ounces)
- 1 tablespoon chicken bouillon dissolved in 1 cup boiling water
- ½ cup dry white wine
- ½ cup heavy cream
- 1 tablespoon Dijon mustard
- 1 tablespoon chopped fresh flat-leaf parsley, for garnish
- Your favorite buttered pasta, rice, or potatoes, for serving (optional)

1. Generously season each chicken breast on both sides with a few pinches each of salt and pepper.

2. Heat the olive oil in a saucepan over medium heat until it just starts to shimmer. Add the chicken breasts to the pan, cooking until golden brown, about 5 minutes, then flip and cook on the other side until golden, another 5 minutes or so. (The chicken doesn't need to be fully cooked as it will finish cooking later.) Once browned, using tongs, remove the chicken from the skillet and transfer to a shallow bowl or rimmed plate to catch any juices that release.

3. In the same skillet, reduce the heat to low and add 2 tablespoons of butter. Add the onion and cook slowly, stirring frequently to prevent burning. Cook until the onion is soft, sweet, and caramelized to a golden brown, about 20 minutes.

4. Once the onion has caramelized, add the remaining 2 tablespoons of butter and the mushrooms and stir. Sauté the mushrooms with the onion until the mushrooms are soft and tender, 10 to 15 minutes, stirring as needed.

5. Next, stir in the water/bouillon mixture and wine, scraping up any brown bits that have accumulated on the bottom of the pan, increase the heat to medium high, and bring the liquid to a simmer. Continue to simmer the sauce until it reduces down by a few tablespoons, then reduce the heat and add the heavy cream and the salt and pepper, and stir to combine. Whisk in the mustard until smooth.

*(recipe continues)*

WEEKNIGHT MEALS

● ● ●

**6.** Create small spaces in the skillet for the chicken breasts and nestle them back into the sauce, adding in any juices that have accumulated on the plate. Reduce the heat to medium, cover the skillet, and let the chicken simmer until it's fully cooked (it should register 165°F on a meat thermometer) and the sauce has thickened to coat the back of a spoon, 10 to 15 minutes. Taste the sauce and add more seasoning as needed. When the chicken is done cooking, if the sauce hasn't thickened enough, remove the chicken, increase the heat, and cook the sauce down until it has thickened more.

**7.** Sprinkle the chicken with the parsley and serve, if using, with your choice of starch, such as rice, pasta, or potatoes. For a more formal presentation, slice the breasts against the grain, and transfer the slices to a platter and drizzle with the sauce, then sprinkle with the parsley. Leftovers can be stored in an airtight container in the refrigerator for up to 4 days.

One thing about me is I. Love. IKEA. If you were an OG YouTube watcher, you know what IKEA and the Alex nine-drawer set meant to me. I love roaming the aisles of the Swedish superstore to check out all the furniture, accessories, deals, and, of course, the restaurant. After I graduated high school, my aunt, who is married to a Swede, took me on a trip to Sweden and the only thing I wanted to do was go to the original nine-story IKEA! This is my aunt's iconic recipe for homemade Swedish meatballs, and they are absolutely better than the ones from that "furniture store."

# "BETTER THAN THAT FURNITURE STORE" SWEDISH MEATBALLS

### Serves 4

- 3 slices fresh white bread
- 1/4 cup whole milk
- 2 tablespoons unsalted butter or extra-virgin olive oil, divided
- 1 medium yellow onion, finely diced (about 1 cup)
- 1 pound ground beef
- 1 pound ground pork
- 3 egg yolks
- 1 1/2 teaspoons kosher salt
- 1/2 teaspoon freshly ground black pepper
- 1/2 teaspoon ground nutmeg
- 1/2 teaspoon ground allspice
- 1 to 2 tablespoons chopped flat-leaf parsley, for garnish
- Crushed red pepper flakes, for garnish (optional)

**1.** Tear the bread into small pieces or pulse it in a food processor (I prefer to put it in the food processor so there aren't any white chunks in my meatballs) and transfer it to a small bowl. Pour the milk over and set aside; the milk won't cover everything and that's fine. (You can add a little more milk if you like a softer meatball, see Remi's Recommendations, page 220.)

**2.** In a large skillet, over medium heat, melt 1 tablespoon of butter. Add the onion and cook, stirring occasionally, until it's softened and just starts to brown on the edges, about 5 minutes. Remove the skillet from the heat and allow the onion to cool.

**3.** In a large bowl, combine the beef, pork, moistened breadcrumbs, egg yolks, salt, black pepper, nutmeg, and allspice. Using your hands, mix the meat with the other ingredients until it's evenly combined.

**4.** Using a tablespoon measure, scoop up a heaping spoonful of the meat mixture (which is actually 2 even tablespoons), roll it into a ball, and place it on a rimmed baking sheet. Repeat this process until all the meat is formed into balls.

*(recipe continues)*

**5.** To cook the meatballs, preheat a large skillet, preferably a nonstick one, over medium heat and pan-fry the meatballs until they are brown on all sides and cooked through, about 10 minutes, cooking them in two batches if necessary as to not crowd the pan. If your skillet is not nonstick or if needed, add the remaining butter for frying.

**6.** Serve the meatballs warm with a sprinkle of the parsley and, if using, red pepper flakes. Leftover meatballs may be stored in an airtight container in the refrigerator for up to 4 days. The meatballs may be reheated in a skillet with a tablespoon or two of water on the stovetop over medium heat until they are heated through, about 10 minutes.

### Remi's Recommendations

If you prefer a softer meatball, you can add more milk. For a firmer meatball, add less bread soaked in milk plus a whole egg instead of just the yolks. The key to a tender meatball, whether it's soft or firm, though, is to *not* overwork the meat. You can do a test by frying up a single meatball in a frying pan and then adjusting the milk or bread until your desired consistency is reached.

### Bake your Meatballs!

Instead of frying your meatballs, bake them on a parchment-lined baking sheet in a 375°F oven for 18 to 20 minutes, until they are cooked through.

I grew up in a house where a rice cooker is a very important appliance, and, more specifically, ours was a Zojirushi rice cooker, which is the Mercedes of rice cookers. While a stovetop pot works just fine, rice cookers ensure perfectly chewy, fluffy grains of rice that never stick or burn. When I moved out of my childhood home, my mom bought me my own rice cooker as my very first housewarming gift (we love our rice cookers). I love set-it-and-forget-it dishes like this one. (When I was younger I'd often forget to take the meat out to thaw when my mom asked me to, so I love anything that can be done ahead!) Inspired by fragrant, velvety Hainanese chicken and rice, this meal serves up comfort in a bowl. It's easy, and while the cooking time may not be superfast, it takes just a few minutes to put it together. You can also cook this dish on the stovetop (see Remi's Recommendations following).

# COMFORTING RICE COOKER GINGER GARLIC CHICKEN

### Serves 4

- 1 cup uncooked sushi rice
- 1 cup water
- ¼ cup soy sauce
- 5 medium green onions (white and green parts separated), white parts coarsely chopped; green parts cut into ½-inch pieces
- 5 garlic cloves, minced or grated
- 1 tablespoon minced or grated fresh ginger
- 2 teaspoons chicken bouillon powder
- Freshly ground black pepper
- 4 boneless, skinless chicken thighs
- Kosher salt
- Flat-leaf parsley, for garnish (optional)
- Toasted sesame oil, for serving

**1.** Put the rice in a fine-mesh strainer and rinse until the water runs clear.

**2.** In your rice cooker, combine the rinsed rice with the water. Stir in the soy sauce, the white parts of the green onions, the garlic, ginger, chicken bouillon, and a few pinches of black pepper. Lay the chicken on top of the rice and other ingredients (try not to disturb the rice when setting the chicken in) and sprinkle the chicken with a few pinches of salt.

**3.** Cook everything together in the rice cooker according to the manufacturer's instructions until the rice is tender and the chicken is cooked through (mine cooks for 1 hour).

**4.** Once done, slice the chicken (or you can also leave it whole), fluff the rice and spoon it onto a platter, top with the chicken, sprinkle with the green parts of the green onions and, if using, parsley, and drizzle with sesame oil. Season with a pinch or two of salt if needed. Serve warm. Leftovers may be stored in an airtight container in the refrigerator for up to 4 days. To reheat, place the chicken and rice in a microwave-safe dish, cover with a damp paper towel, and heat on high until warmed through, 2 to 3 minutes.

*(recipe continues)*

WEEKNIGHT MEALS

● ● ●

### Remi's Recommendations
### Let's Use the Stovetop!

If you don't have a rice cooker, don't fear, you can easily cook this meal in a large pot or Dutch oven on the stovetop. Prepare the recipe as above, but instead of combining everything in a rice cooker, use a large pot or Dutch oven. Over medium-high heat, bring the liquid to a boil, then reduce the heat to low to maintain a very, very slow simmer. Cover and cook until the liquid has absorbed into the rice and the rice is tender and chewy, and the chicken is cooked through, about 45 minutes, then follow the serving instructions in the recipe.

Growing up, my family loved going to Vietnamese restaurants. Because I wasn't super fond of pho at a younger age, discovering bò lúc Lắc, also called shaking beef, was a game-changer. (You shake the pan when cooking the beef!) The juicy bites of meat drenched in an umami-rich soy and oyster sauce quickly became one of my go-to meals. You can easily re-create this dish at home, which I do often for weeknight dinners. It's important to choose a tender cut of meat to get a nice, juicy bite. I like a boneless ribeye or filet mignon, but a strip steak with marbling works well. Also, don't forget the cucumbers and tomatoes, which add that necessary fresh bite!

# VIETNAMESE SHAKING BEEF BOWLS (BÒ LÚC LẮC)

### Serves 2

- 1 (10-ounce) boneless ribeye or filet mignon steak at room temperature, cut into 1-inch cubes
- Kosher salt
- Freshly ground black pepper
- 1 tablespoon neutral oil, such as vegetable or avocado
- ½ medium red onion, thinly sliced
- 2 green onions (white and green parts), cut into 1-inch pieces
- 2 garlic cloves, minced or finely grated
- 2 tablespoons oyster sauce
- 1 tablespoon soy sauce, or more as needed
- 1 teaspoon granulated sugar
- 1 cup cooked white rice, for serving
- 1 tomato, cut into wedges, for serving
- 1 medium cucumber, cut into half-moons, for serving

**1.** Generously sprinkle the steak cubes with salt and pepper.

**2.** Heat the oil in a large skillet over high heat until it shimmers, then add the steak cubes and let them sear on one side until the cubes start to brown on the bottom, 1 to 2 minutes, then "shake" the pan (this is where the shaking comes in!) to turn the steak cubes so they brown on all sides, about another 2 minutes.

**3.** Add the onion, reserving a handful for garnish, the green onions, and garlic to the pan and stir to combine. Cook the vegetables with the meat for 1 minute, shaking as you cook.

**4.** Add in the oyster sauce, 1 tablespoon of soy sauce, and the sugar to the pan. Toss the meat with the sauce to coat. Reduce the heat to medium and continue to cook the mixture, stirring occasionally, until the beef is cooked to your desired doneness and the sauce has caramelized slightly, 3 to 4 minutes for medium rare. Take a taste and add more salt or pepper as needed.

**5.** To serve, remove the pan from the heat and "shake" the beef over a bed of white rice. Garnish with the tomato, cucumber, and the reserved onion slices. Season with more soy sauce if needed. Store leftovers in an airtight container in the refrigerator for up to 4 days.

I've always been a huge peanut fan. Growing up, I'd get so excited when my dad went on business trips because it meant he'd come home with little Southwest Airlines honey-roasted peanut packs from the plane. My early love for those turned me into a fan of all things peanut: peanut M&M's, peanut butter, plain peanuts, and peanut sauce (I could put it on most everything). I find peanut sauce pairs well with proteins (my favorite is chicken), and it's a simple way to upgrade most any weeknight dinner. It takes only minutes to cook chicken thighs, and the sweet-and-salty, creamy sauce, which is my version of a peanut sauce, quickly converts them to an irresistible meal.

# HONEY PEANUT CHICKEN BOWL

### Serves 2 to 3

- 3 tablespoons creamy peanut butter
- 2 tablespoons honey
- 2 tablespoons soy sauce
- 1 tablespoon mirin
- 2 teaspoons rice vinegar
- Kosher salt, for seasoning, if needed
- Freshly ground black pepper, for seasoning, if needed
- 1 tablespoon vegetable oil or other neutral oil
- 4 boneless, skinless chicken thighs (about 1¼ pounds), cut into 1-inch pieces
- 2 garlic cloves, minced or grated
- 1 small head broccoli, cut into florets (about 3 cups)
- 2 to 3 cups cooked white rice, for serving
- ¼ cup dry, unsalted peanuts, chopped

**1.** In a small bowl, whisk together the peanut butter, honey, soy sauce, mirin, and vinegar until smooth. (If your peanut butter does not stir well, warm it in the microwave on high for 30 seconds before adding the other ingredients.) Taste the sauce to see if any additional salt or pepper is needed. Set aside.

**2.** Heat the oil in a medium saucepan over medium heat until it shimmers. Increase the heat to high and add the chicken pieces. Cook, and, using tongs, turn the pieces as they brown so they cook evenly on all sides. Continue to sauté the chicken until no pink remains on the outside, about 3 minutes. Reduce the heat to medium and add the garlic and broccoli and continue to cook, using the tongs to move the chicken and broccoli around, until the broccoli is al dente, about 4 minutes.

**3.** Reduce the heat to low and pour in the prepared peanut sauce, stirring to coat. Continue to cook until all the chicken is cooked through, another 4 minutes or so.

**4.** To serve, divide the rice between 2 or 3 bowls, spoon the chicken, broccoli, and sauce over the rice, sprinkle with the peanuts, and serve warm. Leftovers may be stored in an airtight container in the refrigerator for up to 4 days.

This particular way of preparing salmon feels somewhat elegant (even though it's super easy) and makes it perfect for a date night in. Cal and I have specific spots where we sit around the TV (yes, we are TV dinner people). We want to enjoy each other (and a good show) and not have to worry about cooking for hours, so this quick meal fits right into our routine.

# HONEY MUSTARD-GLAZED SALMON WITH GARLIC PARMESAN ROASTED POTATOES

### Serves 2

**FOR THE POTATOES**

1 pound fingerling potatoes, halved lengthwise
2 tablespoons extra-virgin olive oil
1 teaspoon garlic powder
1 teaspoon onion powder
¼ teaspoon kosher salt
¼ teaspoon freshly ground black pepper
¼ cup grated Parmesan cheese
1 to 2 teaspoons fresh flat-leaf parsley, for garnish

**FOR THE SALMON**

3 tablespoons Dijon mustard
2 tablespoons honey
¼ teaspoon garlic powder
¼ teaspoon onion powder
¼ teaspoon kosher salt
⅛ teaspoon freshly ground black pepper
1 pound skin-on, center-cut salmon fillet, cut into 2 pieces, rinsed and patted dry with a paper towel

**1.** In the oven, arrange 2 racks to accommodate two standard size baking sheets. Preheat the oven to 400°F.

**2.** In a large bowl, toss the fingerling potatoes with the olive oil, garlic powder, onion powder, salt, and pepper until evenly coated.

**3.** Arrange the potatoes flat side down on a rimmed baking sheet.

**4.** Roast the potatoes until golden brown and crispy, flipping them halfway through, 30 to 40 minutes. Once cooked, sprinkle the Parmesan over the hot potatoes and garnish with the fresh parsley.

**5.** Make the salmon: Meanwhile, in a small bowl, whisk together the mustard, honey, garlic powder, onion powder, salt, and pepper. Place the salmon fillets skin-side down on a nonstick or foil-lined baking sheet and brush or spoon the mustard mixture generously over the top of the salmon fillets.

**6.** Bake the salmon until it just starts to become opaque in the center and the fish flakes easily when pulled apart with a fork (or to your desired doneness), 12 to 15 minutes.

**7.** Serve the salmon with the potatoes and any extra honey mustard glaze on the side. Enjoy.

**Remi's Recommendations**

When you are buying salmon, I'd recommend buying the highest-quality fish within your budget. Also, asking for a center-cut fillet ensures that your piece of fish is an even thickness and doesn't include thin parts.

To me, this pasta honestly tastes like I got it at my favorite Italian restaurant. The sauce is so rich and luxurious. The secret? I use the reserved pasta water to thicken the sauce, which results in a silky, creamy texture that coats the noodles quite nicely. I really do think of the starch-rich, salty, cloudy pasta water as liquid gold. Nothing else quite creates that bonding experience between noodles and sauce. This dish is a symphony of flavors you don't want to miss!

# LIQUID GOLD LEMONY SHRIMP LINGUINE

### Serves 2

- 8 ounces dry linguine pasta
- 4 tablespoons (½ stick) unsalted butter, divided
- 1 pound large shrimp, peeled and deveined
- ¼ teaspoon kosher salt, plus more for seasoning
- 1 small shallot, finely diced (about 3 tablespoons)
- 3 garlic cloves, minced or grated
- ¾ cup heavy cream
- ¼ cup freshly squeezed lemon juice
- ⅔ cup shredded Parmesan cheese, plus some shaved for serving (optional)
- 1 teaspoon Italian seasoning
- ¼ teaspoon freshly ground black pepper
- Fresh flat-leaf parsley leaves, for garnish

**1.** Cook the linguine according to package instructions, reserving ¼ cup of the pasta water before draining. Set aside. While the pasta is cooking, prepare the sauce.

**2.** In a large saucepan over medium heat, melt 1 tablespoon of butter and add the shrimp. Sprinkle with a few pinches of salt, and after 1 minute, using tongs, flip the shrimp over. The shrimp will be slightly undercooked at this point but we'll finish cooking them later. Using tongs, transfer the cooked shrimp to a bowl or rimmed plate and set aside.

**3.** In the same pan over medium heat, melt 1 tablespoon of butter and add the shallot, stirring to coat in the butter, and cook them until they are softened, 2 to 3 minutes. Add the garlic and cook another minute or so, or until fragrant.

**4.** Reduce the heat to low and to the shallot and garlic mixture in the pan, stir in the heavy cream, lemon juice, and the remaining 2 tablespoons of butter until combined. Whisk in the ⅔ cup Parmesan, Italian seasoning, the ¼ teaspoon salt, and the pepper.

**5.** Slowly whisk in the reserved pasta water, and let the sauce thicken over low heat while you continue to whisk, another 2 to 3 minutes.

**6.** Add the linguine to the sauce and, using tongs, move the noodles around, pulling them up and down in the sauce until they are well coated. Add the shrimp and toss one more time to coat.

**7.** To serve, garnish the pasta with fresh parsley and, if desired, shaved Parmesan. Shrimp linguine is best eaten right away.

LET'S GET COOKING

I'm not the biggest fan of marinara sauce, but I can't resist vodka sauce! I love the tang of the tomato, the richness of the cheese and cream, and the lusciousness the vodka adds. If you want to skip the vodka, you absolutely can, though. I love making this dish for my girlfriends because it yields a good amount, and they get so excited when they find out it's on the menu. The crispy chicken adds some necessary protein, and extra Parmesan cheese on top is always a must!

# VODKA SAUCE PASTA WITH CRISPY CHICKEN

### Serves 4

**FOR THE PASTA AND SAUCE**

- 1 teaspoon kosher salt, plus more for the pasta water
- 1 pound (16 ounces) dry rigatoni or penne pasta
- 3 tablespoons unsalted butter
- 2 tablespoons extra-virgin olive oil
- 2 large shallots, finely diced (about ½ cup)
- 3 garlic cloves, minced or grated
- 1 (6-ounce) can tomato paste
- ⅓ cup vodka
- ½ cup heavy cream, plus more as needed
- ¼ teaspoon freshly ground black pepper
- 2 teaspoons Italian seasoning
- 1 cup grated Parmesan cheese, plus more for garnish
- Fresh basil leaves, for garnish

**FOR THE CHICKEN**

- 2 boneless, skinless chicken breasts (about 1¼ pounds)
- Kosher salt
- Freshly ground black pepper
- ½ cup all-purpose flour
- 1 teaspoon onion powder, divided
- 1 teaspoon garlic powder, divided
- 2 large eggs

**1.** Bring a large pot of salted water to a boil (add at least 1 tablespoon salt). Once the water has come to a boil, add the pasta and boil until just al dente, 1 to 2 minutes less than the cooking time listed on the package. Before draining, reserve ¾ cup of the pasta water and set the reserved water and the cooked pasta aside (you can leave the pasta in the strainer).

**2.** Make the sauce: In the same large pot that you cooked the pasta, combine the butter and olive oil over low heat until the butter has melted. Add the shallots and cook until translucent, about 4 minutes. Add the garlic and cook until everything just starts to turn golden, another 2 minutes or so. Spoon in the tomato paste and cook, stirring constantly, until it darkens and smells caramelized, 6 to 8 minutes. Add the vodka and stir or whisk until it's incorporated and cook down for several minutes until the alcohol evaporates. Slowly stir in the heavy cream (for a creamier consistency, add up to ¾ cup heavy cream or for a richer tomato taste, only add ⅓ cup). Season with the 1 teaspoon of salt, the pepper, and the Italian seasoning, then stir in ½ cup of the reserved pasta water, bring the sauce to a very slow simmer, and continue to stir, adding more of the reserved water as needed, until the sauce reaches the desired consistency. Stir in the Parmesan and remove from the heat.

**3.** Make the chicken: Place one of the chicken breasts between two pieces of parchment paper and pound it with a mallet until the entire

*(recipe and ingredients continue)*

WEEKNIGHT MEALS

2 cups panko breadcrumbs

2 teaspoons Italian seasoning

1 quart vegetable oil or other high-heat neutral oil, for frying

Basil leaves, for garnish

breast is ⅓-inch thick. Repeat the process with the second breast. Season the chicken all over with a few pinches each of salt and pepper.

**4.** Next, set up your breading stations using 3 shallow bowls. In one, combine the flour with ½ teaspoon salt and ½ teaspoon each of the onion powder and garlic powder. In a second bowl, lightly whisk the eggs until frothy. In the third bowl, combine the breadcrumbs with ½ teaspoon of salt and the remaining ½ teaspoon each of the onion powder and garlic powder, the Italian seasoning, and a few pinches of pepper, stirring to combine.

**5.** With one hand, which we'll call your dry hand, dredge the chicken in the flour to coat, shaking off any excess. Using your other hand, now your "wet" hand, bathe the flour-coated chicken in the egg mixture, thoroughly coating it, then transfer the egg-coated chicken to the breadcrumb bowl. Now using your dry hand, sprinkle the chicken with some breadcrumbs and then fully coat it, pressing the breadcrumbs to fully adhere until the breast is coated. Transfer the breaded cutlet to a large plate or sheet pan and continue the process with the second breast.

**6.** Heat the oil in a large skillet over medium-high heat to 350°F. (You should have about ½-inch of oil in the skillet for a shallow fry, see page 23 for more on frying.) Transfer the breaded chicken to the oil and fry until golden brown and the internal temperature reaches 165°F, flipping halfway through, 4 to 5 minutes per side. Using tongs, transfer the fried cutlets to a paper towel–lined plate and sprinkle with salt and pepper.

**7.** Over low heat, rewarm the pasta sauce, tossing in the cooked pasta until the penne is cooked through and the sauce is warm. Add more pasta water or cream if needed to thin the sauce. When ready to plate, slice the crispy chicken cutlets into strips.

**8.** To serve, divide the pasta into shallow bowls and top with the chicken, then sprinkle with Parmesan, and garnish with a basil leaf. The pasta is best eaten right after cooking. Leftover chicken may be stored in an airtight container in the refrigerator for up to 4 days.

I love pasta! All I need on it is butter and Parm, and I'm happy. This dish, though, elevates traditional buttered pasta to the next level. One simple ingredient—oyster sauce—adds a rich umami flavor to the noods and gives garlic pasta a fun, unexpected Asian-fusion spin.

# GARLIC LOVERS SHRIMP & NOODS

### Serves 4 to 6

Kosher salt

1 pound (16 ounces) dried spaghetti

5 tablespoons unsalted butter, divided

1 tablespoon vegetable oil or other neutral oil

1 pound medium to large shrimp, peeled and deveined

8 garlic cloves, minced, divided

¼ teaspoon freshly ground black pepper, plus more for seasoning

2 tablespoons oyster sauce

1 tablespoon soy sauce

½ cup grated Parmesan cheese, plus more as needed (optional)

1 tablespoon chopped fresh flat-leaf parsley leaves, for garnish

**1.** In a large pot of salted water (add at least 1 tablespoon salt), cook the spaghetti according to the package instructions, drain, and set aside.

**2.** In a large skillet over medium-high heat, combine 2 tablespoons of butter and the oil until the butter has melted. Add the shrimp and half of the minced garlic, sprinkle with 1½ teaspoons salt and the pepper and sauté until the shrimp turns pink and is cooked through, 3 minutes. Transfer the shrimp to a shallow bowl or rimmed plate and set aside.

**3.** In the same skillet over medium heat, melt the remaining 3 tablespoons of butter. Add the remaining minced garlic and cook until fragrant, 1 to 2 minutes. Add the cooked spaghetti to the skillet, and, using tongs, toss the noodles with the butter and garlic until it's fully coated.

**4.** Pour the oyster sauce and soy sauce over the noodles, tossing again to combine. Continue to cook the noodles until they are fully coated in the sauce, 2 to 3 minutes.

**5.** Add the shrimp back to the skillet and season with salt and pepper as needed. Turn off the heat and stir in the Parmesan, mixing until it begins to melt into the noodles.

**6.** To serve, transfer the shrimp and noods to a large serving platter and garnish with fresh parsley and extra Parmesan, if desired. Garlic Lovers Shrimp & Noods are best eaten right after cooking.

That's the **BEST THING** I've ever had in my life!

Inspired by my favorite entrée, Bang Bang Chicken & Shrimp, at the Cheesecake Factory, this super comforting dish combines flavors I love—curry, peanut, chile, and coconut. It's basically my take on a yellow curry, and it's a go-to for me when I want something creamy, comforting, and luscious. You can easily make the curry vegetarian by swapping out the meat for your favorite veggies. In fact, this is another great clean-out-the-fridge recipe (see page 165 for another one) because you can sub in most any meat or veg.

# COCONUT CURRY SHRIMP & CHICKEN BOWL

### Serves 4 to 6

- 3 tablespoons extra-virgin olive oil, divided
- 1 large white onion, cut into ½-inch chunks (about 2 cups)
- 1 green bell pepper, cut into ½-inch chunks
- 1 red bell pepper, cut into ½-inch chunks
- ½ teaspoon kosher salt, divided
- 1 (13.5-ounce) can coconut milk
- 1 tablespoon yellow curry paste
- 1 teaspoon granulated sugar
- 1 teaspoon chicken bouillon powder (optional)
- ¼ teaspoon garlic powder
- 2 boneless, skinless chicken breasts (about 1¼ pounds), cut into ½-inch strips
- 8 ounces large shrimp, peeled and deveined, then rinsed and patted dry
- 2 to 3 cups cooked white rice, for serving
- Fresh cilantro, for garnish

**1.** Heat 1 tablespoon of olive oil in a large saucepan over medium heat until it shimmers. Add the onion and cook for 4 to 5 minutes, stirring, until it becomes translucent. Add the green pepper and red pepper, sprinkle with ¼ teaspoon of salt, and cook, stirring occasionally, until the peppers just start to soften, 3 to 5 minutes. Transfer the cooked onion and peppers to a bowl and set aside.

**2.** In a medium bowl or spouted liquid measuring cup, whisk together the coconut milk, curry paste, sugar, chicken bouillon if using, and the garlic powder until smooth. Set aside.

**3.** Using the same pan over medium-high heat, add the remaining 2 tablespoons of oil and heat until it shimmers. Add the chicken, and, using tongs, move the chicken around, cooking it until no pink is visible (if you cut a strip in half, it should pretty much be cooked through), about 5 minutes. Add the shrimp, sprinkle the remaining ¼ teaspoon of salt over the chicken and shrimp, and cook for 90 seconds, using the tongs to turn the shrimp when they start to turn pink (if needed, add a teaspoon or more of oil to prevent sticking).

**4.** Reduce the heat to low, add the cooked veggies back into the pan, and then pour in the coconut milk/curry paste stir to coat and cook for another minute or two, until everything is warmed through. Taste for seasoning and adjust as needed.

**5.** Serve the curry over rice and garnish with cilantro sprigs. Leftover curry may be stored in an airtight container in the refrigerator for up to 4 days.

WEEKNIGHT MEALS

This twist on classic teriyaki chicken uses inexpensive dark meat, making it both flavorful and budget-friendly. I love using drumsticks because dark meat stays tender and juicy when cooked. Perfect for a casual weeknight meal or a fun party dish, these drumsticks come together easily with simple ingredients. The sweet and savory teriyaki sauce adds a delicious glaze, elevating this dish into a must-make favorite. Cooking them in an air fryer means dinner is ready quickly, and the clean-up is easy.

# AIR FRYER TERIYAKI DRUMSTICKS

### Makes 6 drumsticks

- 1 cup soy sauce
- ½ cup granulated sugar
- ¼ cup mirin
- 3 green onions (white and green parts), thinly sliced
- 3 garlic cloves, minced or grated
- 2 tablespoons grated fresh ginger
- 6 (1½ to 1¾ pounds) chicken drumsticks

**1.** In a saucepan over medium-high heat, combine the soy sauce, sugar, mirin, green onions (reserving 1 to 2 tablespoons for garnish), the garlic, and ginger. Bring the mixture to a boil, then reduce the heat to low and simmer until the sugar has melted, about 1 minute. Remove the marinade from the heat and let it cool completely.

**2.** Place the chicken drumsticks in a large plastic bag or shallow dish and pour the cooled marinade over the drumsticks, ensuring they are well coated. Seal the bag or cover the dish and refrigerate for at least 2 hours, or overnight for the best flavor.

**3.** Preheat your air fryer to 350°F. Remove the drumsticks from the marinade and place them in the air-fryer basket. Cook until the chicken skin is crisp and the chicken is cooked through, 10 to 12 minutes. Remove and place on a serving platter.

**4.** Pour any remaining marinade from the bag or dish into a small saucepan, and, over high heat, bring the mixture to a boil for at least 2 minutes. Reduce the heat to low and simmer until the sauce thickens, 3 to 5 minutes.

**5.** Drizzle the thickened sauce over the cooked drumsticks and garnish with the reserved green onions. Serve with your favorite side dishes, such as steamed rice or a fresh salad. Leftover drumsticks may be stored in the refrigerator for up to 4 days. To reheat, warm in the air fryer preheated to 350°F for 6 to 8 minutes, turning the drumsticks after the first 4 minutes of heating.

### Remi's Recommendations

You can easily bake these drumsticks instead of air frying them. Bake the drumsticks on a foil-lined baking sheet in a 425°F oven until the skin is crisp and the internal temperature is 165°F, 30 to 35 minutes.

# ACKNOWLEDGMENTS

I've been incredibly fortunate to have the most amazing support system around me—this book wouldn't have been possible without them.

First, I want to thank my husband. Cal, you are my rock, my best friend, my everything. Thank you for always being my biggest cheerleader and my number one taste tester. Whenever I got stressed while writing this book, you always knew just how to calm me down or you stepped up and took on more to make things easier for me. Your open-mindedness and willingness to try new things is one of my favorite things about you and was so appreciated throughout this process. I'm so grateful for our experiences we've shared and our travels that inspired so much of this book. I also want to thank the girls—our three dogs, Daisy, Momo, and Luna, who complete our little family. Thank you for providing me the emotional support I need every day. I don't know what I'd do without all of you, and I am the luckiest girl in the world to have you.

To my mom, you've taught me so much of what I know. Watching you create magic in the kitchen while I was growing up is something I will never take for granted. Your ability to try anything and know exactly how to create it and make it better is a skill that I've never seen before. I'm where I am today because of you. You taught me my work ethic, my way of loving, and my love for food. Some of my favorite memories growing up include you making the most delicious dishes for the whole family just because you had the itch to, whether it was homemade fried chicken, soba noodles, or all of your delicious Korean dishes that connected us more to our culture. Thank you for always cheering me on in everything I do. I don't know what I did to be given the most incredible mother who cares with all her heart. I love you.

To my dad, you are truly the best man I've ever known. Thank you for always letting me fly and trusting that I will find my way. I know I can call you anytime, with anything, and you will always drop everything for me. I love you so much.

To Auntie, thank you for all you do. I'll never forget frantically calling you after I moved out on my own and wanting to learn how to make tteokbokki for the first time. You walked me through the whole process and did so again and again whenever I needed a reminder. Thank you for your lifetime of love, patience, and support throughout my whole career. Thank you for all you've taught me—I truly can say I have the best aunt to ever exist.

To the rest of my family—Shane, Uncle Thom, Grandma, Lili, Amy, Tom, Abby, Tyler, and Sam, I appreciate your support more than you know. Thank you for always trying my dishes during the holidays, for the best reactions to my food, and for helping me taste and test these recipes in the book. I love you all so so much!

To my friends—Alisha, Oli, Kaylee, Murph, Mia, Lauren, Chesco, and so many more, thank you all for your constant support in everything I do within work and life. I truly feel like the luckiest girl in the world with the best friends who love me unconditionally. Thank you for always trying all my dishes, helping me with content, and just being the most reliable, fun, loving friends a girl could ask for.

To my team—Tommy, Brooke, Oli, Pranav, Brandi, Whitney, Dan, and Jess, when I say this book wouldn't have happened without you guys, that is not an understatement. I truly don't know how I would have been able to finish this book without all your help. From making the initial proposal, to going to meetings and shopping it around, to helping me get all the ingredients, to sitting with me in the kitchen while I test recipes over and over again. This book is truly a tangible monument of all our hard work. Thank you for being the best team a girl could ask for!

To everyone behind the scenes that has worked so closely with me to bring this book to life—thank you! To the entire team at Simon Element, including Justin Schwartz, Gina Navaroli, and Jen Wang, thank you for walking me through the entire process from start to finish and being patient with me throughout everything. I also want to thank the incredible Rebecca French for her notes, insights, and editorial work. This book would not be what it is without you! To the entire creative team behind all the beautiful imagery throughout the book, it was a dream to work with everyone and see the vision for the book slowly come to life—thank you to Jennifer Chong (photographer), Natalie Drobny (food stylist), Alicia Buszcak (prop stylist), David Peng (photo assistant), Daniela Swamp and Jen Bolbat (food assistants), and Aubrey Devin (prop assistant).

Lastly, to my followers and community, thank you for keeping me with you while we just have fun in the kitchen. Food and cooking don't need to be serious. I love that we can learn together, make mistakes together, and have fun with food together.

# INDEX

## A
Air Fryer Miso-Butter-Glazed Shishito Peppers, 65
Air Fryer Teriyaki Drumsticks, 240, 241
Angel and Deviled Eggs, 80, 81
Apple Pie Breakfast Turnovers, 33-35, 34
Asian Pear Slaw, Korean Fried Chicken Sandwich with, 181-82, 183

## B
Bacon Cheese Dip with Fried Pita Bread, 68-69
Bacony Cheesy Eggy Crunchy Breakfast Wrap, 52-55, 53
Basically Unfiltered (Cruz, podcast), 10
BBB (Best Breakfast Burger), 130, 131-32
beef
    "Better Than That Furniture Store" Swedish Meatballs, 218, 219-20
    Galbi-Jjim (Braised Beef Short Rib Stew), 171-72, 173
    Galbi (Korean Short Rib) Breakfast Burritos, 30, 31-32
    Galbi (Marinated Short Ribs), 168, 169-70
    short ribs, flanken vs. English-style, 20
    Vietnamese Shaking Beef Bowls, 224, 225
Best-Ever Garlic Butter Rolls, 89
Best Turkey Burger You'll Ever Have, 208, 209, 210, 211
"Better Than That Furniture Store" Swedish Meatballs, 218, 219-20
beverages
    Cal's Salted Caramel Cold Foam Espresso Martini, 60, 61
    Chocolate-Covered Strawberry Smoothie, 46, 47
    Strawberry Lemonade Tequila Batch Cocktail, 58, 62, 63
Biscuits, Homemade, and Sage Sausage Gravy, 136, 137-38
boiling eggs, 23
Braised Beef Short Rib Stew (Galbi-Jjim), 171-72
bread
    Best-Ever Garlic Butter Rolls, 89
    breadcrumbs, about, 24
    breadcrumbs, in Crunchy Street Dogs, 155-56, 157
    French Toast with Homemade Whipped Cream, Crunchy Cereal, 121-22, 123
    Fried Pita Bread, Bacon Cheese Dip with, 68-69
    Homemade Biscuits and Sage Sausage Gravy, 136, 137-38
breakfast. see grab-and-go breakfasts
Brown Butter Sugar Cookies, 108, 109-10
brunch. see weekend drunchie brunch
Brussels Sprouts, Smashed Parmesan-Crusted, 76, 77
Brussels Sprouts, Sweet Chili Fried Salmon Bites with Hot Honey, 196, 197
Budae-Jjigae (Korean Army Stew) Crispy Potstickers, 152, 153-54
Buffalo Chicken-Stuffed Sweet Potatoes, 204-5
Butternut Squash Soup, Cozy, 201-2, 203

## C
Cal's Salted Caramel Cold Foam Espresso Martini, 60, 61
Caramel (date), for Ooey Gooey Chocolate Caramel Candy Bars, 111-12, 113
Caramelized Onion Chicken with Mushrooms, 215-16, 217
Caramelized Onion Dip, 66, 67
cheese
    Bacon Cheese Dip with Fried Pita Bread, 68-69

**245**

cheese (cont.)
- Bacony Cheesy Eggy Crunchy Breakfast Wrap, 52-55, *53*
- in Best-Ever Garlic Butter Rolls, 89
- Cheesy Jalapeño Poppers, 72
- Cheesy Kimchi Pork Belly Panini, *141,* 166, *167*
- Crispy Cheddar Hash Brown Avocado Toast, 118-20, *119*
- Korean Cheesy Corn Casserole, 186, *187*
- Korean Street-Style Ham and Cheese Sandwiches with Sweet Sriracha Mayo, *184,* 185
- Mango and Brie Cheesy Quesadillas, 195
- Party-Pleaser Goat Cheese-Stuffed Dates, *70,* 71

chicken
- Air Fryer Teriyaki Drumsticks, 240, *241*
- Buffalo Chicken-Stuffed Sweet Potatoes, 204-5
- Caramelized Onion Chicken with Mushrooms, 215-16, *217*
- Coconut Curry Shrimp & Chicken Bowl, *238,* 239
- Comforting Rice Cooker Ginger Garlic Chicken, 221-22, *223*
- Cruz Family's Famous Chicken Tenders, *212,* 213-14
- Garlic Parmesan Chicken Wings, *94,* 95-96
- in Get Your Gains Sausage Egg Bites, 43-44
- Honey Peanut Chicken Bowl, 226, *227*
- Japanese Air-Fried Chicken Bites, 92, *93*
- Korean Fried Chicken Sandwich with Asian Pear Slaw, 181-82, *183*
- Soy Garlic Hot Honey Chicken Wings, 147-49, *148*
- Vodka Sauce Pasta with Crispy Chicken, *232,* 233-34

chocolate
- Chocolate-Covered Strawberry Smoothie, *46,* 47
- Galaxy Brownie Overnight Oats, *50,* 51
- Ooey Gooey Chocolate Caramel Candy Bars, 111-12, *113*
- World's Best Cakey Chocolate Chip Cookies, *102,* 103-4

Cocktail, Strawberry Lemonade Tequila Batch, *58, 62,* 63
Coconut Chia Pudding, Hot Girl, *28, 29, 48, 49*
Coconut Curry Shrimp & Chicken Bowl, *238,* 239
Comforting Rice Cooker Ginger Garlic Chicken, 221-22, *223*
Cookies, Brown Butter Sugar, *108,* 109-10
Cookies, World's Best Cakey Chocolate Chip, *102,* 103-4
cooking techniques. *see also* ingredients
- boiling eggs, 23
- breadcrumbs, 24
- deep frying, 23-24
- hot honey, 24
- rice cookers, 221
- sweet sriracha mayo, 24
- thermometers, 23-24

@CookingWithRemi (Cruz, cooking series), 10
Cozy Butternut Squash Soup, 201-2, *203*
Crab Cake Eggs Benedict with Homemade Hollandaise, *115,* 127-29, *129*
Crispy Cheddar Hash Brown Avocado Toast, 118-20, *119*
Crispy Rice Salad, *206,* 207
Crispy Tempura Green Beans with Garlic Aioli, *78,* 79
Croissant Breakfast Bake, 139
Crunchy Breakfast Wrap, Bacony Cheesy Eggy, 52-55, *53*
Crunchy Cereal French Toast with Homemade Whipped Cream, 121-22, *123*
Crunchy Street Dogs, 155-56, *157*
Cruz, Remi
- about, 10-11
- favorite recipes of, 25, 143 (*see also* Korean dish favorites)

Cruz Family's Famous Chicken Tenders, *212,* 213-14

## D

dates
- in Ooey Gooey Chocolate Caramel Candy Bars, 111-12, *113*
- Party-Pleaser Goat Cheese-Stuffed Dates, *70,* 71

deep frying, 23-24
desserts
- Brown Butter Sugar Cookies, *108,* 109-10
- Hot Girl Coconut Chia Pudding, *28, 29, 48, 49*
- Out-of-This-World Galaxy Brownies, 105-6, *107*
- Sweetest Strawberry Butter Cake Bars, *56-57,* 97-98, *99, 100, 101*
- World's Best Cakey Chocolate Chip Cookies, *102,* 103-4

Deviled Eggs, Angel and, 80, *81*
dips and dipping sauce
- Bacon Cheese Dip with Fried Pita Bread, 68-69
- Caramelized Onion Dip, *66,* 67

Dipping Sauce, for Budae-Jjigae (Korean Army Stew) Crispy Potstickers, *152,* 153-54

## E

eggs
  about, boiling, 23
  Angel and Deviled Eggs, 80, *81*
  Bacony Cheesy Eggy Crunchy Breakfast Wrap, 52-55, *53*
  boiling eggs, 23
  Crab Cake Eggs Benedict with Homemade Hollandaise, *115,* 127-29, *129*
  Get Your Gains Sausage Egg Bites, 43-44
  Kimchi Fried Rice with an Egg, *164,* 165
  Korean Soy-Marinated Eggs, 150, *151*
English-style short ribs, 20
Espresso Martini, Cal's Salted Caramel Cold Foam, 60, *61*

## F

favorite dishes. *see* Korean dish favorites
flanken short ribs, 20
French Toast with Homemade Whipped Cream, Crunchy Cereal, 121-22, *123*
fridge ingredients, 13, *14-15*. *see also* ingredients
Fried Crab Rangoons with Sweet Chili Sauce, *90,* 91
Fried Pita Bread, Bacon Cheese Dip with, 68-69
frostings. *see* toppings (for desserts and sweet dishes)
fruit
  Apple Pie Breakfast Turnovers, 33-35, *34*
  Chocolate-Covered Strawberry Smoothie, *46,* 47
  in Liquid Gold Lemony Shrimp Linguine, *191,* 230, *231*
  Mango and Brie Cheesy Quesadillas, 195
  Strawberry Lemonade Tequila Batch Cocktail, *58,* 62, *63*
  Sweetest Strawberry Butter Cake Bars, *56-57,* 97-98, *99, 100, 101*
  Fruity-Flavored Cereal Milk-Glazed Pancakes, *116, 117,* 133-34, *135*

## G

Galaxy Brownie Overnight Oats, *50,* 51
Galbi-Jjim (Braised Beef Short Rib Stew), 171-72, *173*
Galbi (Korean Short Rib) Breakfast Burritos, *30,* 31-32
Galbi (Marinated Short Ribs), *168,* 169-70
garlic
  about, 11
  Best-Ever Garlic Butter Rolls, 89
  Comforting Rice Cooker Ginger Garlic Chicken, 221-22, *223*
  Crispy Tempura Green Beans with Garlic Aioli, *78,* 79
  Garlic Lovers Shrimp & Noods, *189,* 235, *237*
  Garlic Parmesan Chicken Wings, *94,* 95-96
  Hawaiian Garlic Shrimp, *192,* 193-94
  Honey Mustard-Glazed Salmon with Garlic Parmesan Roasted Potatoes, *228,* 229
  Roasted Japanese Sweet Potato Soup with Garlicky Croutons, *198,* 199-200
  Soy Garlic Hot Honey Chicken Wings, 147-49, *148*
  Get Your Gains Sausage Egg Bites, 43-44
  Ginger Garlic Chicken, Comforting Rice Cooker, 221-22, *223*
glazes. *see* toppings (for entrees and side dishes)
gochugaru, 19
Gochujang Meatballs, Sweet and Spicy, *142, 178,* 179-80
gochujang paste, 19
grab-and-go breakfasts, 26-55
  about, 29
  Apple Pie Breakfast Turnovers, 33-35, *34*
  Bacony Cheesy Eggy Crunchy Breakfast Wrap, 52-55, *53*
  Chocolate-Covered Strawberry Smoothie, *46,* 47
  Galaxy Brownie Overnight Oats, *50,* 51
  Get Your Gains Sausage Egg Bites, 43-44
  Hot Girl Coconut Chia Pudding, *28, 29,* 48, *49*
  Korean Short Rib (Galbi) Breakfast Burritos, *30,* 31-32
  Quick & Easy Monkey Bread Muffins, *26, 27, 36, 37, 38-39*
  Savory Surprise Breakfast Muffins, *40,* 41-42
gravy, for Homemade Biscuits and Sage Sausage Gravy, *136,* 137-38
Green Beans with Garlic Aioli, Crispy Tempura, *78,* 79

## H

ham and cheese, in Best-Ever Garlic Butter Rolls, 89

INDEX **247**

Ham and Cheese Sandwiches with Sweet Sriracha Mayo, Korean Street-Style, *184,* 185
hard-boiled eggs, 23
Hawaiian Garlic Shrimp, *192,* 193-94
Hollandaise Sauce, for Crab Cake Eggs Benedict, *115,* 127-29, *129*
Homemade Biscuits and Sage Sausage Gravy, *136,* 137-38
honey
    Honey Mustard-Glazed Salmon with Garlic Parmesan Roasted Potatoes, *228,* 229
    Honey Peanut Chicken Bowl, 226, *227*
    hot honey, about, 24
    Hot Honey Brussels Sprouts, Sweet Chili Fried Salmon Bites with, 196, *197*
    Miso Honey-Glazed Sea Bass Cups, *82,* 83-84
    Soy Garlic Hot Honey Chicken Wings, 147-49, *148*
hosting, recipes for parties. *see* party recipes
Hot Girl Coconut Chia Pudding, *28, 29,* 48, *49*

**I**

ingredients
    author's use of, 11
    beef, flanken vs. English-style short ribs, 20
    fridge and pantry, 13, *14–15*
    gochugaru, 19
    gochujang paste, 19
    kimchi, 19
    mirin, 20
    oils, 24
    plum extract syrup, 20
    pork belly, 20, 154
    rice vinegar, 20
    shopping for, 19
    soy sauce, 20
    toasted sesame oil, 20

**J**

Jalapeño Poppers, Cheesy, 72
Japanese Air-Fried Chicken Bites, 92, *93*

**K**

kimchi
    about, 19
    Cheesy Kimchi Pork Belly Panini, *141,* 166, *167*
    Kimchi Fried Rice with an Egg, *164,* 165
    Kimchi Slaw, for Korean Short Rib (Galbi) Breakfast Burritos, *30,* 31-32
    Mom's Kimchi-Jjigae (Kimchi Stew), *174, 175,* 176, *177*
Korean dish favorites, 140-87
    about, 25, 143
    Budae-Jjigae (Korean Army Stew) Crispy Potstickers, *152,* 153-54
    Cheesy Kimchi Pork Belly Panini, *141,* 166, *167*
    Crunchy Street Dogs, 155-56, *157*
    Galbi-Jjim (Braised Beef Short Rib Stew), 171-72, *173*
    Galbi (Marinated Short Ribs), *168,* 169-70
    Kimchi Fried Rice with an Egg, *164,* 165
    Korean Buffalo Cauliflower Bites, *158,* 159-60
    Korean Cheesy Corn Casserole, 186, *187*
    Korean Fried Chicken Sandwich with Asian Pear Slaw, 181-82, *183*
    Korean Soy-Marinated Eggs, 150, *151*
    Korean Street-Style Ham and Cheese Sandwiches with Sweet Sriracha Mayo, *184,* 185
    Mom's Kimchi-Jjigae (Kimchi Stew), *174, 175,* 176, *177*
    Rosé Udon with Crispy Pork Belly, 161-62, *163*
    Soy Garlic Hot Honey Chicken Wings, 147-49, *148*
    Sweet and Spicy Gochujang Meatballs, *142, 178,* 179-80
    Tteokbokki (Spicy Stir-Fried Rice Cakes), *144,* 145-46

**L**

Liquid Gold Lemony Shrimp Linguine, *191,* 230, *231*

**M**

Mango and Brie Cheesy Quesadillas, 195
marinades. *see* toppings (for entrees and side dishes)
Martini, Cal's Salted Caramel Cold Foam Espresso, 60, *61*
Matcha Latte Pancakes, *124,* 125-26
meat and meatballs. *see also* beef; pork
    "Better Than That Furniture Store" Swedish Meatballs, *218,* 219-20
    Crunchy Street Dogs, 155-56, *157*
    Super-Easy Slow Cooker Meatballs, 85
    Sweet and Spicy Gochujang Meatballs, *142, 178,* 179-80
menus, for party recipes, 64. *see also* party recipes

mirin, 20
Miso Honey-Glazed Sea Bass Cups, *82,* 83-84
@MissRemiAshten, (Cruz, YouTube channel), 10
Mom's Kimchi-Jjigae (Kimchi Stew), *174, 175,* 176, *177*
Mushrooms, Caramelized Onion Chicken with, 215-16, *217*

# N

noodles and pasta
    Budae-Jjigae (Korean Army Stew) Crispy Potstickers, *152,* 153-54
    Garlic Lovers Shrimp & Noods, *189,* 235, *237*
    Liquid Gold Lemony Shrimp Linguine, *191,* 230, *231*
    Vodka Sauce Pasta with Crispy Chicken, *232,* 233-34

# O

oils, 24
onion
    Caramelized Onion Chicken with Mushrooms, 215-16, *217*
    Caramelized Onion Dip, *66,* 67
    onion powder, 11
Ooey Gooey Chocolate Caramel Candy Bars, 111-12, *113*
Out-of-This-World Galaxy Brownies, 105-6, *107*
Overnight Oats, Galaxy Brownie, *50,* 51

# P

Pancakes, Fruity-Flavored Cereal Milk-Glazed, *116, 117,* 133-34, *135*
Pancakes, Matcha Latte, *124,* 125-26

panko, 24
pantry ingredients, 13, *14-15. see also* ingredients
Party-Pleaser Goat Cheese-Stuffed Dates, *70,* 71
party recipes, 56-113
    about, 59, 64
    Air Fryer Miso-Butter-Glazed Shishito Peppers, 65
    Angel and Deviled Eggs, 80, *81*
    Bacon Cheese Dip with Fried Pita Bread, 68-69
    Best-Ever Garlic Butter Rolls, 89
    Brown Butter Sugar Cookies, *108,* 109-10
    Cal's Salted Caramel Cold Foam Espresso Martini, 60, *61*
    Caramelized Onion Dip, *66,* 67
    Cheesy Jalapeño Poppers, 72
    Crispy Tempura Green Beans with Garlic Aioli, *78,* 79
    Fried Crab Rangoons with Sweet Chili Sauce, *90,* 91
    Garlic Parmesan Chicken Wings, *94,* 95-96
    Japanese Air-Fried Chicken Bites, *92, 93*
    Miso Honey-Glazed Sea Bass Cups, *82,* 83-84
    Ooey Gooey Chocolate Caramel Candy Bars, 111-12, *113*
    Out-of-This-World Galaxy Brownies, 105-6, *107*
    Party-Pleaser Goat Cheese-Stuffed Dates, *70,* 71
    Smashed Parmesan-Crusted Brussels Sprouts, 76, *77*
    Spicy Salmon and Avocado on Crispy Rice, 73-75, *74*
    Strawberry Lemonade Tequila Batch Cocktail, *58, 62,* 63

Super-Easy Slow Cooker Meatballs, 85
Suz's Cornflake Potato Casserole, *86,* 87-88
Sweetest Strawberry Butter Cake Bars, *56-57, 97-98, 99, 100, 101*
World's Best Cakey Chocolate Chip Cookies, *102,* 103-4
Peanut Chicken Bowl, Honey, 226, *227*
Pear Puree, for Galbi-Jjim (Braised Beef Short Rib Stew), 171-72
Pear Slaw, Asian, Korean Fried Chicken Sandwich with, 181-82, *183*
peppers
    Air Fryer Miso-Butter-Glazed Shishito Peppers, 65
    Cheesy Jalapeño Poppers, 72
    in condiments, 19, 24
    in Sweet and Spicy Gochujang Meatballs, *142, 178,* 179-80
    Sweet Chili Fried Salmon Bites with Hot Honey Brussels Sprouts, 196, *197*
    Sweet Chili Sauce, Fried Crab Rangoons with, *90,* 91
plum extract syrup, 20
pork and ham. *see also individual bacon entries*
    "Better Than That Furniture Store" Swedish Meatballs, *218,* 219-20
    Budae-Jjigae (Korean Army Stew) Crispy Potstickers, *152,* 153-54
    Cheesy Kimchi Pork Belly Panini, *141,* 166, *167*

INDEX **249**

pork and ham (*cont.*)
    ham and cheese, in Best-Ever Garlic Butter Rolls, 89
    Homemade Biscuits and Sage Sausage Gravy, *136,* 137-38
    Korean Street-Style Ham and Cheese Sandwiches with Sweet Sriracha Mayo, *184,* 185
    pork belly, about, 20, 154
    Rosé Udon with Crispy Pork Belly, 161-62, *163*
Powdered Sugar Glaze, for Quick & Easy Monkey Bread Muffins, 36
Pretty Basic (Cruz, podcast), 10
Pudding, Hot Girl Coconut Chia, *28, 29,* 48, *49*

## Q

Quick & Easy Monkey Bread Muffins, *26, 27,* 36, *37, 38-39*

## R

@RemLife (Cruz, YouTube channel), 10
rice
    in Comforting Rice Cooker Ginger Garlic Chicken, 221-22, *223*
    Crispy Rice Salad, *206,* 207
    Kimchi Fried Rice with an Egg, *164,* 165
    rice vinegar, about, 20
    Spicy Salmon and Avocado on Crispy Rice, 73-75, *74*
    Tteokbokki (Spicy Stir-Fried Rice Cakes), *144,* 145-46
rice cookers, about, 221
Roasted Japanese Sweet Potato Soup with Garlicky Croutons, *198,* 199-200
Rosé Udon with Crispy Pork Belly, 161-62, *163*

## S

salmon
    Honey Mustard-Glazed Salmon with Garlic Parmesan Roasted Potatoes, *228,* 229
    Spicy Salmon and Avocado on Crispy Rice, 73-75, *74*
    Sweet Chili Fried Salmon Bites with Hot Honey Brussels Sprouts, 196, *197*
Salted Caramel Cold Foam Espresso Martini, Cal's, 60, *61*
sauces. *see* toppings (for desserts and sweet dishes); toppings (for entrees and side dishes)
Sausage Egg Bites, Get Your Gains, 43-44
Sausage Gravy, Sage, Homemade Biscuits and, *136,* 137-38
Savory Surprise Breakfast Muffins, *40,* 41-42
Sea Bass Cups, Miso Honey-Glazed, *82,* 83-84
seafood
    Coconut Curry Shrimp & Chicken Bowl, *238,* 239
    Crab Cake Eggs Benedict with Homemade Hollandaise, *115,* 127-29, *129*
    Fried Crab Rangoons with Sweet Chili Sauce, *90,* 91
    Garlic Lovers Shrimp & Noods, *189,* 235, *237*
    Hawaiian Garlic Shrimp, *192,* 193-94
    Honey Mustard-Glazed Salmon with Garlic Parmesan Roasted Potatoes, *228,* 229
    Liquid Gold Lemony Shrimp Linguine, *191,* 230, *231*
    Miso Honey-Glazed Sea Bass Cups, *82,* 83-84
    Spicy Salmon and Avocado on Crispy Rice, 73-75, *74*
    Sweet Chili Fried Salmon Bites with Hot Honey Brussels Sprouts, 196, *197*
sesame oil, toasted, 20
Shishito Peppers, Air Fryer Miso-Butter-Glazed, 65
short ribs, flanken vs. English-style, 20. *see also* beef
shrimp
    Coconut Curry Shrimp & Chicken Bowl, *238,* 239
    Garlic Lovers Shrimp & Noods, *189,* 235, *237*
    Hawaiian Garlic Shrimp, *192,* 193-94
    Liquid Gold Lemony Shrimp Linguine, *191,* 230, *231*
Simple Syrup, for Cal's Salted Caramel Cold Foam Espresso Martini, 60, *61*
Smashed Parmesan-Crusted Brussels Sprouts, 76, *77*
Smoothie, Chocolate-Covered Strawberry, *46,* 47
soft-boiled eggs, 23
soups and stews
    Budae-Jjigae (Korean Army Stew) Crispy Potstickers, *152,* 153-54
    Cozy Butternut Squash Soup, 201-2, *203*
    Galbi-Jjim (Braised Beef Short Rib Stew), 171-72, *173*
    Mom's Kimchi-Jjigae (Kimchi Stew), *174,* 175, 176, *177*
    Roasted Japanese Sweet Potato Soup with Garlicky Croutons, *198,* 199-200

soy
- Air Fryer Miso-Butter-Glazed Shishito Peppers, 65
- Air Fryer Teriyaki Drumsticks, 240, *241*
- Korean Soy Marinated Eggs, 150, *151*
- Miso Honey-Glazed Sea Bass Cups, *82*, 83-84
- Soy Garlic Hot Honey Chicken Wings, 147-49, *148*
- soy sauce, about, 20

Spicy Salmon and Avocado on Crispy Rice, 73-75, *74*
Spicy Stir-Fried Rice Cakes (Tteokbokki), *144*, 145
Strawberry Butter Cake Bars, Sweetest, *56-57*, 97-98, *99*, *100*, *101*
Strawberry Lemonade Tequila Batch Cocktail, *58*, *62*, 63
Strawberry Smoothie, Chocolate-Covered, *46*, 47
Super-Easy Slow Cooker Meatballs, 85
Suz's Cornflake Potato Casserole, *86*, 87-88
Sweet and Spicy Gochujang Meatballs, *142*, *178*, 179-80
Sweet Chili Fried Salmon Bites with Hot Honey Brussels Sprouts, 196, *197*
Sweet Potatoes, Buffalo Chicken-Stuffed, 204-5
sweet sriracha mayo, about, 24
Sweet Sriracha Mayo, Korean Street-Style Ham and Cheese Sandwiches with, *184*, 185

# T

Teriyaki Drumsticks, Air Fryer, 240, *241*
thermometers, 23-24
toasted sesame oil, 20
toppings (for desserts and sweet dishes)
- Caramel (date)/Topping, for Ooey Gooey Chocolate Caramel Candy Bars, 111-12, *113*
- Cream, for Matcha Latte Pancakes, *124*, 125-26
- Frosting, for Out-of-This-World Galaxy Brownies, 105-6, *107*
- Glaze, for Fruity-Flavored Cereal Milk-Glazed Pancakes, 116, *117*, 133-34, *135*
- Powdered Sugar Glaze, for Quick & Easy Monkey Bread Muffins, 36

toppings (for entrees and side dishes)
- Dipping Sauce, for Budae-Jjigae (Korean Army Stew) Crispy Potstickers, *152*, 153-54
- Dressing, for Crispy Rice Salad, *206*, 207
- gravy, for Homemade Biscuits and Sage Sausage Gravy, *136*, 137-38
- Hollandaise Sauce, for Crab Cake Eggs Benedict, *115*, 127-29, *129*
- Hot Honey Brussels Sprouts, Sweet Chili Fried Salmon Bites with, 196, *197*
- in Korean Fried Chicken Sandwich with Asian Pear Slaw, 181-82, *183*
- in Miso Honey-Glazed Sea Bass Cups, *82*, 83-84
- Pear Puree, for Galbi-Jjim (Braised Beef Short Rib Stew), 171-72
- sauce, for Soy Garlic Hot Honey Chicken Wings, 147-49, *148*
- sauce, for Tteokbokki (Spicy Stir-Fried Rice Cakes), *144*, 145

Tteokbokki (Spicy Stir-Fried Rice Cakes), *144*, 145-46
turkey
- The Best Turkey Burger You'll Ever Have, 208, *209*, *210*, *211*
- Sweet and Spicy Gochujang Meatballs, *142*, *178*, 179-80

# V

vegetables. *see also* kimchi; onion
- Cozy Butternut Squash Soup, 201-2, *203*
- Crispy Tempura Green Beans with Garlic Aioli, *78*, 79
- Garlic Parmesan Roasted Potatoes, Honey Mustard-Glazed Salmon with, *228*, 229
- Hot Honey Brussels Sprouts, Sweet Chili Fried Salmon Bites with, 196, *197*
- Roasted Japanese Sweet Potato Soup with Garlicky Croutons, *198*, 199-200
- Smashed Parmesan-Crusted Brussels Sprouts, 76, *77*
- Suz's Cornflake Potato Casserole, *86*, 87-88
- Sweet Potatoes, Buffalo Chicken-Stuffed, 204-5

Vietnamese Shaking Beef Bowls, *224*, 225
Vodka Sauce Pasta with Crispy Chicken, *232*, 233-34

## W

weekend drunchie brunch, 114–39
  about, 117
  BBB (Best Breakfast Burger), *130*, 131–32

weekend drunchie brunch (*cont.*)
  Crab Cake Eggs Benedict with Homemade Hollandaise, *115*, 127–29, *129*
  Crispy Cheddar Hash Brown Avocado Toast, 118–20, *119*
  Croissant Breakfast Bake, 139
  Crunchy Cereal French Toast with Homemade Whipped Cream, 121–22, *123*
  Fruity-Flavored Cereal Milk-Glazed Pancakes, *116*, *117*, 133–34, *135*
  Homemade Biscuits and Sage Sausage Gravy, *136*, 137–38
  Matcha Latte Pancakes, *124*, 125–26

weeknight meals, 188–241
  about, 190
  Air Fryer Teriyaki Drumsticks, 240, *241*
  The Best Turkey Burger You'll Ever Have, 208, *209*, *210*, *211*
  "Better Than That Furniture Store" Swedish Meatballs, *218*, 219–20
  Buffalo Chicken-Stuffed Sweet Potatoes, 204–5
  Caramelized Onion Chicken with Mushrooms, 215–16, *217*
  Coconut Curry Shrimp & Chicken Bowl, *238*, *239*
  Comforting Rice Cooker Ginger Garlic Chicken, 221–22, *223*
  Cozy Butternut Squash Soup, 201–2, *203*
  Crispy Rice Salad, *206*, *207*
  Cruz Family's Famous Chicken Tenders, *212*, 213–14
  Garlic Lovers Shrimp & Noods, *189*, 235, *237*
  Hawaiian Garlic Shrimp, *192*, 193–94
  Honey Mustard–Glazed Salmon with Garlic Parmesan Roasted Potatoes, *228*, *229*
  Honey Peanut Chicken Bowl, 226, *227*
  Liquid Gold Lemony Shrimp Linguine, *191*, 230, *231*
  Mango and Brie Cheesy Quesadillas, 195
  Roasted Japanese Sweet Potato Soup with Garlicky Croutons, *198*, 199–200
  Sweet Chili Fried Salmon Bites with Hot Honey Brussels Sprouts, 196, *197*
  Vietnamese Shaking Beef Bowls, *224*, *225*
  Vodka Sauce Pasta with Crispy Chicken, *232*, 233–34

Whipped Cream, Homemade, Crunchy Cereal French Toast with, 121–22, *123*

World's Best Cakey Chocolate Chip Cookies, *102*, 103–4

## Y

YouTube, author's channels on, 10

### YouTube
Vlog Channel: @RemLife
Main Channel: @MissRemiAshten

### Instagram
Main: @MrsRemiAshten
Cooking: @CookingWithRemi

### TikTok
@MissRemiAshten

### Online
CookingWithRemi.com

An Imprint of Simon & Schuster, LLC
1230 Avenue of the Americas
New York, NY 10020

For more than 100 years, Simon & Schuster has championed authors and the stories they create. By respecting the copyright of an author's intellectual property, you enable Simon & Schuster and the author to continue publishing exceptional books for years to come. We thank you for supporting the author's copyright by purchasing an authorized edition of this book.

No amount of this book may be reproduced or stored in any format, nor may it be uploaded to any website, database, language-learning model, or other repository, retrieval, or artificial intelligence system without express permission. All rights reserved. Inquiries may be directed to Simon & Schuster, 1230 Avenue of the Americas, New York, NY 10020 or permissions@simonandschuster.com.

Copyright © 2026 by Remi Cruz

Photography Copyright © 2026 by Jennifer Chong

Food Stylist: Natalie Drobny
Prop Stylist: Alicia Buszcak
Photo Assistant: David Peng
Food Assistants: Daniela Swamp and Jen Bolbat
Prop Assistant: Aubrey Devin

All rights reserved, including the right to reproduce this book or portions thereof in any form whatsoever. For information, address Simon Element Subsidiary Rights Department, 1230 Avenue of the Americas, New York, NY 10020.

First Simon Element hardcover edition March 2026

SIMON ELEMENT is a registered trademark of Simon & Schuster, LLC

Simon & Schuster strongly believes in freedom of expression and stands against censorship in all its forms. For more information, visit BooksBelong.com.

For information about special discounts for bulk purchases, please contact Simon & Schuster Special Sales at 1-866-506-1949 or business@simonandschuster.com.

The Simon & Schuster Speakers Bureau can bring authors to your live event. For more information or to book an event, contact the Simon & Schuster Speakers Bureau at 1-866-248-3049 or visit our website at www.simonspeakers.com.

Interior design by Janet Evans-Scanlon

Manufactured in China

10 9 8 7 6 5 4 3 2 1

Library of Congress Cataloging-in-Publication Data has been applied for.

ISBN 978-1-6680-6683-6
ISBN 978-1-6680-6684-3 (ebook)

Let's stay in touch! Scan here to get book recommendations, exclusive offers, and more delivered to your inbox.